THE OFFICIAL COOKBOOK

CANDY LAND

THE OFFICIAL COOKBOOK

More than 50 Recipes for Delicious Treats, Decorations,
and Activities Inspired by the Beloved Board Game!

Kristy Richardson

INSIGHT
EDITIONS

SAN RAFAEL · LOS ANGELES · LONDON

CONTENTS

INTRODUCTION

Sweet chocolate bubbles and flows down a river that is winding right beside cool whipped mountain tops. It rushes past the colorful path where Gingerbread Movers skip quickly toward a colorful castle covered in gooey gumdrops, peppermint swirls, and sweet sprinkles.

CANDY LAND is a magical place full of delicious treats! King Kandy and Queen Frostine welcome you and can't wait to share all of their favorite sweet, colorful, and even sparkly treats that have been created in CANDY LAND!

Start your journey in CANDY LAND in an extra sweet way! Syrupy **Cinnamon Swirl French Toast (page 11)** and **King Kandy's Bagel Sandwiches (page 15)**, which are famously pink, are the best way to greet the day.

Next, in the cookies chapter, make some **Gingerbread Movers Cookies (page 36)** that can take you straight down the rainbow path, but be sure to pause for some gooey **Peanut Butter Cup S'mores (page 31)**. They are out-of-this-world delicious!

Sweetness turns up an extra notch in the cakes and cupcakes chapter with a **Sprinkle Explosion Cake (page 42)** so full of rainbows and cheer that you won't be able to help but smile. King Kandy takes a pause to sample Duchess E. Claire's decadent **Mini Double Chocolate Raspberry Tarts (page 52)**, which are fit for any royal tea party.

Next cruise through CANDY LAND for a nibble of **Ice Cream Bonbons (page 64)**, just like you'd find scattered in the Ice Cream Peaks, or the sweetest sip of a **Cherrific Ice Cream Float (page 71)**. In the candy-based chapter, make the **Ultimate Caramel Apple Lollipops (page 84)**—they're so tall! Or swirl a little extra minty sparkle into the beautiful **Double Minty White Chocolate Bark (page 86)**.

Wash it all down with a **Sweet Cotton Candy Sipper (page 111)**, perfect for parties. Or make some **Dreamy Whipped Cream (page 99)** and top a treat with **Homemade Sprinkles (page 96)** made in your favorite color.

Don't forget to invite your friends to CANDY LAND! King Kandy and Queen Frostine have some amazing party and decoration tips that can make any CANDY LAND party extra enchanting! Make your lips pop with **Sprinkle Lips (page 118)**, and turn your party into a candy wonderland with the **Jumbo Wrapped Candy Party Decoration (page 121)**.

Grab a whisk and some sweet ingredients, then get ready for a CANDY LAND adventure in the kitchen to share with all of your family and friends!

TOP-NOTCH TIPS FOR COOKING LIKE A PRO

Whether you're new to cooking or a home-grown pro, it's always a good idea to brush up on the basics. Here are some helpful pointers for practicing kitchen safety while you're cooking.

STAY SAFE!

The best chefs know that safety is the most important thing when it comes to creating yummy treats. Here's what to know before rolling up your sleeves:

- Always ask an adult for help when you have questions or need assistance, especially when using the stove top, oven, and kitchen appliances, and whenever you need to use a knife or other sharp tools.

- Be extra careful with sharp knives and tools.

- Wash your hands with warm soapy water before cooking or handling ingredients.

- Remember to tie back your hair if it's long to keep it out of the way.

- Always stay in the kitchen if you have something on the stove top or in the oven. It's a good idea to set a timer so you don't forget to check if your dish is ready.

- Use thick, dry oven mitts when handling anything that is hot in order to protect your hands from burns. (Wet mitts or towels will burn!)

- Let hot pans cool before moving them to the sink or washing them.

- While it's tempting to sample baked goodies hot from the oven, don't forget to follow any cooling instructions in the recipe.

Astronaut Alan Shepard made a peanut butter and jelly sandwich in space in the International Space Station. His sandwich was made of peanut butter, strawberry jam, and a tortilla, and he ate it in zero gravity.

CHAPTER 1
BREAKFAST

Skip the snooze button and start your day in the sweetest way with breakfast! A CANDY LAND breakfast is worth getting out of bed for. You'll jump for joy with these gooey, decadent, and sweet breakfast ideas. Whether you are having a lazy Saturday morning, celebrating a holiday, or waking up early to greet the sun, you will find delicious breakfast treats here.

Start your day extra sweet with delicious treats, such as Cinnamon Swirl French Toast **(page 11)**, Gooey Chocolate Falls Porridge **(page 21)**, or Sweet PB&J Waffle Sandwiches **(page 22)**. We can learn how to make whipped sweet cream cheese, how to crimp pastry, and how to make a custard for French toast. King Kandy can't wait to start his day with these delicious treats.

CINNAMON SWIRL FRENCH TOAST

With swirls of sweet, dreamy cinnamon and sugar atop thick slices of French toast that melt in your mouth, this is King Kandy's favorite breakfast at Candy Castle. Rich and delicious, garnish this sweet breakfast with maple syrup, whipped cream, powdered sugar, or a drizzle of Gooey Chocolate Sauce (page 95) straight from Chocolate Falls.

YIELD: 2 SERVINGS

4 large eggs

½ cup milk

½ teaspoon pure vanilla extract

4 thick slices cinnamon swirl bread (older bread works best!)

1 tablespoon salted butter

POPULAR TOPPINGS

Maple syrup

Dreamy Whipped Cream (page 99)

Powdered sugar

Fresh fruit

Gooey Chocolate Sauce (page 95)

Homemade Strawberry Sauce (page 105)

In a medium bowl, combine the eggs, milk, and vanilla. Whisk together with a whisk or fork. Place the bread in a shallow baking dish large enough to fit all four slices side by side.

Pour the egg mixture over the bread and let it set for 10 minutes. Turn the bread over and let it sit until most of the liquid has been absorbed into the bread.

Heat a large frying pan or flat-top griddle over medium heat until warm. Working in batches as needed, place about a quarter of the butter per bread slice in the pan, letting it melt and spreading the butter around the pan.

Add the soaked bread slices in a single layer. Cook for about 2 minutes, until the bottom of the bread is golden brown. Flip the bread over and cook for about 2 more minutes, until the second side is golden and the center puffs slightly, then remove the French toast from the pan.

Serve and enjoy with any or all of the popular toppings!

Cinnamon comes from the bark of a tree, which can grow over sixty feet tall.

Cinnamon sticks are called quills.

SWEET STRAWBERRY JAM TOASTER TARTS

Sweet strawberry jam mini tarts drizzled with just the right amount of glaze—these enchanting toaster tarts burst with strawberry flavor in every bite. King Kandy loves the strawberry version, but sometimes he swaps in other flavors of jam, such as blueberry, peach, and raspberry! These handmade tarts are best heated on their side in a toaster oven or pan, but your taste buds will be rewarded!

YIELD: 12 TARTS

FOR THE DOUGH

2 cups all-purpose flour, plus more for dusting

¼ cup powdered sugar

½ teaspoon salt

10 tablespoons unsalted butter, cut into pieces

1 large egg yolk

⅓ cup plus 2 tablespoons whole milk

FOR THE FILLING

2 teaspoons cornstarch

1 teaspoon cold water

¾ cup strawberry jam (or your favorite flavor)

2 large eggs, beaten

2 teaspoons warm water

FOR THE GLAZE

1 cup powdered sugar

2 teaspoons whole milk

2 teaspoons corn syrup

½ teaspoon pure vanilla extract

Sprinkles, for decoration (optional)

To make the dough: In a food processor, combine the flour, ¼ cup powdered sugar, and salt. Pulse until the ingredients are well blended. Add the butter and continue pulsing until the mixture resembles thick crumbs. Add one egg yolk and ⅓ cup plus 2 tablespoons whole milk and pulse until a dough just forms.

Turn the dough out onto two large sheets of overlapping plastic wrap. Press the dough into a ball and refrigerate for at least 30 minutes. This dough can also rest in the refrigerator overnight.

To make the filling: While the dough is chilling, in a small bowl, mix the cornstarch with the water. In a small saucepan over medium heat, combine the jam and the cornstarch mixture. Cook, stirring, for 1 to 2 minutes, until slightly thickened and bubbling. Remove the jam from the heat and let it cool completely.

Next, fill the tarts. Line two baking sheets with parchment paper and remove the dough from the refrigerator. On a lightly dusted work surface, divide the dough in half. Form each half into a rectangle as best as you can.

Roll one rectangle until it measures about 16 by 9 inches. With a sharp knife, carefully cut the dough into twelve 3-by-4-inch rectangles. Set the rectangles on a prepared baking sheet and refrigerate for just a few minutes while you repeat with the other piece of dough.

Lay half of the rectangles on the work surface. In a small bowl with a fork, beat together two eggs and warm water. Use a silicone brush to lightly brush the edges of each piece of dough with the egg mixture. Add a tablespoonful of the filling into the center of each piece of dough. Spread out the jam but leave a ½-inch border around the edge of each rectangle to close the toaster tarts.

Top each tart with another piece of dough. Carefully press the edges of the dough together without pushing the filling out. Push a fork down around the edges to crimp the dough together and seal the tarts. Repeat with the second half of the dough to make the other half of the tarts. Brush the tops of the tarts with any remaining egg mixture.

Put finished tarts on the prepared baking sheets, leaving 2 to 3 inches between each tart. Prick the top of the tarts all over with a fork. Refrigerate while preheating the oven to 375°F.

Bake the tarts for 15 to 18 minutes, or until golden brown. Carefully transfer them to a wire rack and allow to cool completely.

To make the glaze: While the tarts cool, in a medium bowl, combine the powdered sugar, 2 teaspoons of whole milk, corn syrup, and vanilla. Mix with a whisk or a fork until smooth. Spread the glaze on the tarts evenly with a spoon. Decorate with sprinkles (if using) and enjoy!

> Jam is made from pureed, mashed, and cooked fruit while jelly is made from only fruit juice.

KING KANDY'S BAGEL SANDWICHES

Hungry for a sandwich? King Kandy has an amazing open-faced sandwich that everyone loves berry much! Start with mini bagels, add a swirl of sweet homemade strawberry cream cheese, then top with colorful sprinkles, diced strawberries, or both. King Kandy knows it's the berry best!

YIELD: 6 SANDWICHES

4 ounces cream cheese, softened

2 tablespoons honey

⅛ teaspoon pure vanilla extract

5 to 6 strawberries, diced (about ¾ cup), plus more for serving

6 mini bagels or 4 regular bagels

Sprinkles, for serving

Fairy bread is the name for sliced bread with butter and sprinkles, and it is a common treat for kids in Australia and New Zealand.

Place the cream cheese in a large bowl. With an electric mixer on medium speed, whip the cream cheese for about 1 minute. Add the honey and vanilla and whip again until mixed.

Add strawberries and mix again until well combined. You can leave the strawberries in fruity pieces or whip longer to fully mix. Refrigerate for 10 to 15 minutes to firm up the cream cheese. Make this up to a day in advance, but place in an airtight container if storing for more than half an hour.

To serve, halve the mini bagels, toast, and allow to cool. Spread the strawberry cream cheese onto each bagel, about 1 tablespoon per half bagel. Top with more strawberries, sprinkles, or both, then enjoy!

CREAMY YOGURT SUNDAE PARFAITS

Queen Frostine loves a cool creamy treat, and this parfait is the dreamiest! Topped with sweet fruits and granola for crunch, these treats are making waves just like the ones in Sundae Lake. Give the top of the yogurt a good stir and this parfait will give you an extra skip in your step to start the day!

YIELD: 2 SUNDAES

1 cup vanilla yogurt

2 tablespoons honey

¼ teaspoon pure vanilla extract

¼ cup diced strawberries

¼ cup blueberries

¼ cup blackberries

¼ cup diced kiwi

¼ cup fresh orange juice

½ cup granola, divided

In a small bowl, stir together the yogurt, honey, and vanilla.

In a medium bowl, combine the strawberries, blueberries, blackberries, and kiwi. Add the orange juice and stir gently until mixed.

Set out two large clear juice glasses or two 8-ounce mason jars. In each glass, layer a quarter of the yogurt mixture followed by a quarter of the fruit mixture and then a quarter of the granola. Repeat the layers, ending with the granola.

Serve at once or cover and refrigerate for up to 3 hours before serving, then enjoy!

SPRINKLE MAGIC SILVER DOLLAR PANCAKES

Jolly never misses the chance to add a dash of color and sweet to a meal, and these mini pancakes explode with fun! These fluffy pancakes filled with colorful sprinkles are stacked as high as the Gumdrop Mountains, then topped with a creamy whipped cream and sweet berries. Dig your fork into these colorful pancake stacks perfect for your breakfast plate.

YIELD: 24 TO 26 MINI PANCAKES

1 cup all-purpose flour

2 tablespoons granulated sugar

2 teaspoons baking powder

1 teaspoon baking soda

Pinch salt

1 cup milk

1 large egg

2 tablespoons unsalted butter, melted

¼ teaspoon pure vanilla extract

¼ cup rainbow jimmies, plus more for topping

Nonstick cooking spray or salted butter, for greasing

Dreamy Whipped Cream (page 99)

Maple or chocolate syrup, for serving

Berries, for serving

Preheat the oven to 250°F. Line a baking sheet with parchment paper.

In a large bowl, stir together the flour, granulated sugar, baking powder, baking soda, and salt.

In a medium bowl with a whisk, mix together the milk, egg, butter, and vanilla. Pour the milk mixture into the flour mixture and whisk until smooth. With a silicone spatula, fold in the jimmies.

Heat a griddle pan or large frying pan over medium heat. Lightly grease the pan with nonstick cooking spray. Using a tablespoon, work in batches and drop small rounds of batter onto the pan. Cook the pancakes, turning them at least once, for 2 to 3 minutes, until both sides are golden brown. Transfer the pancakes to a baking sheet and keep them warm in the oven. Grease the pan as needed with more cooking spray.

Layer stacks of pancakes to serve. Top with whipped cream and more sprinkles, then add berries and chocolate or maple syrup, if desired, and enjoy!

Gumdrop Mountains

GOOEY CHOCOLATE FALLS PORRIDGE

Gooey chocolate mixed with chewy oats is Duchess E. Claire's grand breakfast idea that everyone loves! Chocolate for breakfast? Yes, please! Creamy, chocolaty oats are just the start. Top your porridge with sweet fruit and crunchy almonds for a delicious breakfast. Just grab a spoon and dig in!

YIELD: 2 TO 3 SERVINGS

3 cups water

1¾ cups old-fashioned rolled oats

1 cup milk or nondairy milk of choice

Pinch of salt

3 tablespoons brown sugar

2 tablespoons unsweetened cocoa powder

2 bananas, sliced (optional)

10 to 12 raspberries (optional)

Sliced almonds, for garnish

In a medium-deep pan over high heat, combine the water, oats, milk, and salt. Bring the mixture to a gentle boil, stirring gently and occasionally with a wooden spoon or spatula while cooking.

As soon as the oats begin to boil quickly, turn the heat down to medium-low to keep the pan at a simmer. Cook the oats for 7 to 8 minutes, continuing to occasionally stir. The oat mixture will absorb the liquid and thicken. Gently blow on the oats and taste to make sure they are tender. Stir in the brown sugar and cocoa powder.

To serve, portion the porridge into two to three bowls. Sprinkle each bowl with sliced bananas (if using), a few raspberries (if using), and sliced almonds, then enjoy!

Chocolate comes from a fruit tree and is made from the seed of the tree. A cacao seed is about the same size as a papaya.

Chocolate Falls

21

SWEET PB&J WAFFLE SANDWICHES

Sweet jam swirled together with creamy peanut butter piled high on a fluffy waffle will make a gooey sandwich you may need a knife and fork to eat. King Kandy himself has made sure every bite of these waffles is gooey, delicious, and sure to enchant all of your family and friends

YIELD: 4 TO 6 WAFFLES

Nonstick cooking spray, for greasing

2 large eggs

1½ cups milk

1 cup smooth peanut butter, divided

4 tablespoons unsalted butter, melted

1½ cups all-purpose flour

3 tablespoons granulated sugar

1 tablespoon baking powder

½ teaspoon salt

1 cup jam, jelly, or preserves of choice

SPECIALTY TOOLS

Waffle iron

Heat a waffle iron and grease with nonstick cooking spray if your model calls for it.

In a large bowl, combine the eggs, milk, ½ cup of peanut butter, and the butter. With an electric mixer on medium speed, whip the mixture together until smooth, about 2 minutes.

In a medium bowl, combine the flour, granulated sugar, baking powder, and salt. Add the flour mixture to the peanut butter mixture. With the mixer on low speed, mix until a smooth batter forms, with no dry bits remaining.

Using a ⅓- to ½-cup measure, pour the batter into the waffle iron. (Follow your model's instructions. For example, if you have a Belgian waffle iron, you may need ¾ cup of batter per waffle.)

Spread the batter starting in the center so that it almost reaches the edges of the hot waffle iron. Cook for 3 to 4 minutes, until the waffle is crisp and brown. Carefully remove the waffle from the waffle iron and repeat with the remaining batter.

Place the jam in a small microwave-safe bowl. Heat in the microwave for about 30 seconds, or until the jam is just gently warmed and pourable.

To serve, halve regular waffles or quarter large Belgian waffles. Place a waffle piece on a plate and spread some of the remaining peanut butter on top. With a spoon, add some of the warm jam, then top with another waffle slice. Enjoy!

The average American will eat three thousand peanut butter and jelly sandwiches in their lifetime.

The thickness of jam come from pectin, which naturally occurs in fruit, but is brought out by adding sugar and cooking the fruit.

CHAPTER 2
COOKIES

■ ■ ■

Cookies are the life of the party and perfect for sharing! Make sweet, buttery, and gooey cookies just because or for a special occasion, such as a birthday or sleepover, or just because it's Monday.

In this chapter, try cookies like Choco-Lct Butter Cookies **(page 29)**, Jam Swirl Cookie Wheels **(page 33)**, or Gingerbread Movers Cookies **(page 36)**, which are always on the run! We'll make cutout cookies, make cookie dough into colorful twists, and learn ways to add flavors inside of cookies.

Queen Frostine loves these cookies and sometimes makes the round cookies extra sweet by creating delectable cookie sandwiches with a little ice cream or Dreamy Whipped Cream **(page 99)** in between! When she is feeling extra magical, Queen Frostine rolls the edges of the cookie sandwiches in sprinkles for a pretty final touch.

CANDY CANE COOKIES

◼◼◼

Fresh from the Peppermint Forest, Mayor Mint carefully watches each candy cane grow tall. These candy cane sugar cookies have just the right amount of cool vanilla and sweet peppermint, all wrapped up in a buttery cookie—the most minty creation from the Peppermint Forest! Mayor Mint adds a sprinkle of crushed peppermint candy or colorful sanding sugar right after baking for the sweetest finish to these delicious cookies.

YIELD: 24 COOKIES

2½ cups all-purpose flour, plus more for dusting

1 teaspoon baking powder

½ teaspoon salt

1 cup (2 sticks) unsalted butter, softened

¾ cup granulated sugar

3 large egg yolks

1½ teaspoons pure vanilla extract

1 teaspoon peppermint extract

Red food coloring (gel food coloring works best)

1½ tablespoons crushed peppermint candies (optional)

1½ tablespoons white or red sanding sugar (optional)

In a medium bowl, mix together the flour, baking powder, and salt, then set aside.

In a large bowl with an electric mixer on medium speed, cream the butter and granulated sugar until light and fluffy, about 3 minutes. Reduce the speed to low and add the egg yolks one at a time, mixing well after each addition. Add the vanilla and mix until combined. Scrape the sides of the bowl with a silicone spatula.

Add the flour mixture a little at a time to the butter mixture and mix on low speed until a dough forms, about 1 minute.

Divide the dough into two equal pieces. Place one dough ball back in the bowl. Add the peppermint extract and a couple of drops of red food coloring to the center of the dough. Mix with an electric mixer until completely combined and the dough changes color. If needed, add more food coloring until the dough is the desired shade of red. Now you have one red peppermint dough piece and one plain dough piece.

Shape each dough piece into a ball and wrap tightly in plastic wrap. Refrigerate the dough overnight.

Preheat the oven to 350°F. Line two baking sheets with parchment paper.

Let the dough balls soften on the counter until it rolls easily. On a lightly dusted work surface, roll out each dough ball to a ¼-inch thickness. Cut each piece of dough into strips that are about 6 inches long and ¾ inch wide (a pizza cutter and a large cutting board works great). Combine the scraps of like colors together, then reroll and cut again as needed.

Take one red strip and one plain strip of dough, then pinch one side's ends together. Gently twist the red and plain strips around each other and pinch the other ends to secure the dough. Bend one end into a hook to form a candy cane shape. Repeat until all the dough is used.

Place each cookie about 1½ inches apart on the prepared baking sheets. Bake for about 8 minutes, until the cookies are just golden on the edges. Remove from the oven and immediately sprinkle the cookies with the crushed peppermint and sanding sugar (if using).

Transfer the cookies to a wire rack, let cool, then enjoy.

The first peppermint sticks were straight in shape and didn't have the iconic hook on the end that we've come to expect today.

CHOCO-LOT BUTTER COOKIES

Could King Kandy ever choose between chocolate and vanilla? Why choose when you can have both! Crumbly, rich, and buttery vanilla cookies dipped in chocolate make one delicious treat. You'll love these sweet dipped butter cookies a choco-lot!

YIELD: 10 COOKIES

1 cup all-purpose flour

¾ cup cake flour

½ teaspoon salt

12 tablespoons (¾ cup) unsalted butter, softened

½ cup powdered sugar

1 teaspoon pure vanilla extract

½ cup semisweet chocolate chips

> Chocolate melts in your mouth because it melts at 93°F, which is less than what your body temperature is (98.6°F).

In a medium bowl, combine the all-purpose flour, cake flour, and salt.

In a large bowl with an electric mixer on medium speed, cream the butter, powdered sugar, and vanilla until smooth, 1 to 2 minutes.

Add the flour mixture to the butter mixture and mix on low speed just until a dough forms. Shape the dough into a ball and wrap tightly in plastic wrap. Chill the dough for at least 1 hour until firm and up to overnight.

Preheat the oven to 350°F and line two baking sheets with parchment paper.

Lightly flour a clean work surface, then roll out the dough with a rolling pin until it is about ¼ inch thick. Use a 2-inch round cookie cutter to cut out cookies. Transfer the cookies to the prepared baking sheets, leaving 1 inch between cookies.

Bake for 14 to 15 minutes, until the cookies are just golden brown at the edges. Place a piece of parchment paper or wax paper under a wire cookie rack. Transfer the cookies to the wire rack to cool.

Place the chocolate chips in a heatproof bowl. Melt the chocolate in 20- to 30-second intervals in the microwave, stirring between each one, until the chocolate is smooth, 2 to 3 minutes.

Dip half of each cookie into the chocolate, then place the cookie back on the wire rack. If you are concerned about your dipping skills, drizzle the chocolate over top of the cookies while on the wire rack.

Allow the chocolate to set and firm up before storing. Store in an airtight container at room temperature for up to five days.

PEANUT BUTTER CUP S'MORES

Golden brown marshmallows filled with gooey centers on top of peanut butter cups? Duchess E. Claire could hardly wait to show Queen Frostine when she came up with this delicious combination! The whole palace enjoyed a magical campfire next to Chocolate Falls, packed with songs and smiles. Everyone cheered for the combination of gooey peanut butter, marshmallows, and chocolate! S'mores are traditionally prepared over a campfire outdoors, as described here, but parents can help children make these over a gas stove or charcoal grill, if desired, too.

YIELD: 12 S'MORES

12 large marshmallows

12 large peanut butter cups

12 whole graham crackers, halved into squares

SPECIAL TOOLS:

Campfire stick

Pierce a marshmallow onto the tip of a campfire stick. Let the kids hold the marshmallows over the embers of a campfire to roast them, turning them constantly, for 3 to 4 minutes, or until golden brown on all sides.

To make each s'more, place a peanut butter cup on a graham cracker square. Top the peanut butter cup with a roasted marshmallow, then place a second graham cracker square on top of the marshmallow. Gently squish the graham crackers together just a little to make a gooey sandwich.

The name s'more stands for "give me some more." The word *s'more* was made popular by the Girl Scouts. The recipe of toasting marshmallows and combining them with chocolate and graham crackers was first written down in the 1927 *Girl Scout Handbook*.

BONUS! Sugar and Spice:
If you're feeling adventurous, try these variations:

1. Use mini chocolate mint patties or chocolate-covered caramels instead of peanut butter cups.

2. Try white chocolate bars or dark chocolate bars in place of peanut butter cups.

3. Swap regular graham crackers for chocolate or cinnamon graham crackers.

4. Use chocolate-hazelnut spread in place of peanut butter cups.

5. Try coconut-coated, stuffed, or chocolate-covered marshmallows.

JAM SWIRL COOKIE WHEELS

While hiking is Jolly's favorite way to enjoy the Gumdrop Mountains, these sweet cookie wheels can go, go, go! These tasty jam cookies are efficient at not only being delicious but also getting him to where he needs to go. Swirl your cookies with strawberry jam (or your favorite flavor of jam) to give them that extra vroom-vroom in the middle of the delicious buttery flavor!

YIELD: 30 COOKIES

3 cups all-purpose flour, plus more for dusting

1 teaspoon baking powder

½ teaspoon salt

1 cup (2 sticks) unsalted butter, softened

1¼ cups granulated sugar

1 large egg

2 teaspoons pure vanilla extract

1 tablespoon heavy cream

2 cups strawberry jam, divided

¼ cup white or red sanding sugar

Jam made from oranges is called marmalade and is made with the fruit and peels. Curd is made from cooked down citrus juice, but it also includes sugar, butter, and sometimes cream or eggs.

In a medium bowl, mix together the flour, baking powder, and salt.

In a large bowl with an electric mixer on medium speed, cream the butter and granulated sugar until light and fluffy, about 3 minutes. Add the egg and vanilla and beat on low speed until they are completely mixed in.

Add the flour mixture a little at a time to the butter mixture and continue to mix on low speed until a dough begins to form. Add the cream and beat until just combined. Scrape down the sides of the bowl with a silicone spatula as needed.

Preheat the oven to 350°F. Line two baking sheets with parchment paper.

On a lightly dusted work surface, roll the cookie dough into a 16-by-12-inch rectangle that is about ¼ inch thick. Spread the jam over the dough, leaving a ½-inch border around the edges. Starting at the long end, tightly roll up the dough until you reach the end and your rolling has formed a long log.

Use a knife to trim any uneven ends. Refrigerate or freeze the dough until firm, about 15 minutes.

Using a sharp knife, cut the roll along the short side into thirty ½-inch-thick slices. Carefully transfer the slices to the prepared baking sheets, leaving 1½ inches between each cookie. Sprinkle each cookie with white sanding sugar for a sweet finish.

Bake for 16 to 19 minutes, until the cookies are just lightly golden around the edges. Transfer the cookies to a wire rack to cool, then enjoy!

CONFETTI COOKIES

When King Kandy bounces into the throne room for a jubilee, these confetti cookies are on the first plate that's brought to his celebratory feast. Soft and cakey, these gooey cookies have a colorful explosion inside. While King Kandy loves them all by themselves, he is even more enchanted when a dollop of vanilla ice cream is sandwiched between two cookies!

YIELD: 12 COOKIES

1½ cups all-purpose flour

⅛ teaspoon baking powder

⅛ teaspoon baking soda

⅛ teaspoon salt

6 tablespoons unsalted butter, softened

¼ cup vegetable shortening

½ cup plus 2 tablespoons granulated sugar

1 large egg

1 large egg yolk

1½ teaspoons pure vanilla extract

2 tablespoons heavy cream

½ cup rainbow sprinkles

The name *cookie* comes from the Dutch word *koekje*, which means "small cake." When baking a cake, people would use a little of the batter to test the oven temperature and make sure it was hot enough before baking the whole cake.

Preheat the oven to 350°F. Line two baking sheets with parchment paper.

In a medium bowl, combine the flour, baking powder, baking soda, and salt. Set aside.

In a large bowl with an electric mixer on medium speed, cream the butter, shortening, and granulated sugar until light and fluffy, about 3 minutes. Add the whole egg plus the egg yolk and the vanilla. Mix together on low speed until completely combined. Scrape down the sides of the bowl with a silicone spatula as needed.

Add the flour mixture to the butter mixture a little at a time. With an electric mixer on low speed, mix the dough just until blended. Add the cream and mix until just combined. With a silicone spatula, fold in the sprinkles until well mixed.

Add the dough in tablespoon-size balls onto the prepared baking sheets, leaving about 2 inches between each dough ball.

Bake for 11 to 12 minutes, until the cookies are golden brown around the edges and lightly golden in the center.

Let the cookies cool for about 5 minutes on the baking sheets to finish cooking, then transfer to a wire rack to cool completely. Enjoy!

GINGERBREAD MOVERS COOKIES

Gingerbread Movers are the name of the game, and they're always on the move! Help these Gingerbread Movers race down the rainbow CANDY LAND path, past the Chocolate Falls and the lollipops in Lollipop Lane. Then sprint with your movers down through the Peppermint Forest, around the Ice Cream Peaks, and all the way to the Candy Castle to be the winner! Decorate these gingerbread cookies with different eyes, noses, glasses, and button shapes so you can tell them apart on the game board or on your cookie tray.

YIELD: 30 COOKIES

3 cups all-purpose flour, plus more for dusting

1 teaspoon baking soda

½ teaspoon baking powder

½ teaspoon salt

1½ teaspoons ground ginger

1½ teaspoons ground cinnamon

1 teaspoon ground allspice

1 cup (2 sticks) unsalted butter, softened

1¼ cups firmly packed light brown sugar

1 large egg

2 tablespoons molasses

1 tablespoon finely grated fresh ginger

Homemade Sprinkles (page 96), made with modifications (see following page)

In a bowl, whisk together the flour, baking soda, baking powder, salt, ground ginger, cinnamon, and allspice.

In a large bowl with an electric mixer on medium speed, cream the butter and brown sugar until light and fluffy, about 3 minutes. Add the egg, molasses, and fresh ginger. Beat on a low speed until thoroughly combined.

Add the flour mixture a little at a time to the butter mixture. Continue to mix until just combined, scraping the bowl with a silicone spatula as needed.

Form the dough into a rectangle, then wrap tightly in plastic wrap. Refrigerate until firm, at least 1 hour and up to overnight. (The dough can also be wrapped well and frozen for up to 1 month and still taste fresh!)

Preheat the oven to 350°F. Line two baking sheets with parchment paper.

Lightly dust a clean work surface with flour. With a dusted rolling pin, roll the chilled dough until it's about ¼ inch thick. Use cookie cutters shaped like gingerbread men to cut the dough.

Combine the scraps together, roll out the dough again, and cut out more cookies. Place the cookies on the prepared baking sheets with at least 1 inch between them.

Bake for 12 to 15 minutes, or until the cookies are soft but not gooey in the center. Let the cookies cool for a few minutes on the pan, then transfer them to wire rack to cool completely.

Use the recipe for Homemade Sprinkles on page 96 for the frosting. Instead of drying it out, place the frosting in a piping bag or zip-top bag with a small hole cut out of the corner. Use this frosting to decorate the cookies. Enjoy!

The first known cookie was made in Persia in the seventh century. Cookies became more common when sugar was introduced into the area.

Originally, gumdrops were flavored with spices, including cinnamon, allspice, spearmint, anise (black licorice), clove, peppermint, and wintergreen.

COOKIE FLOWER POPS

The sun was shining when Princess Lolly discovered her cookie flower pops were in full bloom. A gift from King Kandy and Queen Frostine to add even more sweetness to Lollipop Lane, these flower pops make her want to burst into a happy song every time she sees the sweet petals. These buttery sweet cookie pops will quickly go from bud to full bloom in your kitchen!

YIELD: 12 COOKIE FLOWERS

FOR THE COOKIES

2⅓ cups all-purpose flour, plus more for dusting

¼ teaspoon baking powder

⅛ teaspoon salt

1 cup (2 sticks) unsalted butter, softened

⅔ cup granulated sugar

1 large egg

1½ teaspoons pure vanilla extract

FOR THE ICING

1 cup powdered sugar

1 tablespoon plus 1 teaspoon fresh lemon juice

2 to 3 drops food coloring of choice

Americans eat an average of eighteen thousand cookies in their lifetime.

To make the cookies: In a medium bowl, combine the flour, baking powder, and salt, then set aside.

In a large bowl with an electric mixture on medium-high speed, cream the butter and granulated sugar until super fluffy, about 5 minutes. Add the egg and vanilla and mix until well combined.

Add the flour mixture, a little at a time, to the butter mixture. Continue to mix on low speed until just combined, scraping the bowl with a silicone spatula as needed.

Shape the dough into a ball and wrap tightly in plastic wrap. Refrigerate the dough until firm, at least 1 hour but up to overnight.

Preheat the oven to 350°F. Line two baking sheets with parchment paper.

On a lightly dusted work surface, roll out the dough ball to a ¼-inch thickness. Use flower-shaped cookie cutters to cut cookies from the dough, then place them on the prepared baking sheets spaced about 1½ inches apart. Carefully insert a wooden craft stick into the thin edge of a flower petal.

Bake for 15 to 20 minutes, until the cookies are golden brown. Let the cookies cool briefly on the pan, then transfer them to wire racks to cool completely.

To make the icing: In a small bowl with a spoon, mix together the powdered sugar, lemon juice, and food coloring until smooth.

Decorate the cooled cookies with the icing and enjoy!

CHAPTER 3
CAKES AND CUPCAKES

When it's time to celebrate big with cheers, King Kandy rolls out his favorite cakes and cupcakes. Crazy, over the top, yummy, and delicious cakes and cupcakes make a huge statement that just screams, "Let's party!" Whether you're celebrating a birthday, a holiday, or getting good grades, a showstopping cake or cupcake becomes the highlight of any day!

Recipes like Sparkle Mountain Cupcakes (page 46), Sprinkle Explosion Cake (page 42), and PB&J Cupcakes (page 51) are meant for sharing sweet moments. Learn how to roll a cake with a twist.

Be bold and add your own little extra spin when you are decorating your cake or cupcakes. Additions like a few extra sprinkles, an extra drizzle of gooey chocolate sauce, or a pretty cherry on top can make your dessert shine even more!

SPRINKLE EXPLOSION CAKE

Magical celebrations call for magical cakes topped with a sweet, colorful explosion of fun, frosting, and sprinkles! Queen Frostine loves this cake when it's time to celebrate anything sweet in CANDY LAND, and it goes so well with a scoop of your favorite frosty ice cream. Long, skinny sprinkles, sometimes called jimmies, work better inside this cake than round, hard nonpareil sprinkles, which can bleed when added to the cake batter. However, you can decorate the outside with any sprinkles you want!

Note: Use rainbow jimmies inside the cake but any sprinkles can be used on the outside for decoration.

YIELD: 10 SERVINGS

FOR THE SPRINKLE EXPLOSION CAKE

3¼ cups all-purpose flour, plus more for dusting

1 tablespoon baking powder

1 teaspoon baking soda

¾ teaspoon salt

¾ cup whole milk

½ cup buttermilk

¾ cup water

1 cup (2 sticks) unsalted butter, softened, plus more for greasing

1¾ cups granulated sugar

1 tablespoon pure vanilla extract

3 large eggs

1 cup rainbow jimmies

FOR THE BUTTERCREAM FROSTING

1 cup (2 sticks) unsalted butter, softened

6 cups powdered sugar

1 tablespoon pure vanilla extract

¼ cup heavy cream

1 cup rainbow jimmies or sprinkles of choice

To make the cake: Preheat the oven to 325°F. Lightly butter and flour the sides of three 8-inch round cake pans. Line the bottom of each pan with a circle of parchment paper to make sure the cakes come out of the pans smoothly.

In a medium bowl, combine the flour, baking powder, baking soda, and salt.

In a glass 2-cup measuring cup, combine the whole milk, buttermilk, and water.

In a large bowl with an electric mixer on medium speed, cream the butter and granulated sugar until light and fluffy, about 3 minutes. Add the vanilla and mix until fully combined. Add the eggs, one at a time, beating well after each addition.

With the mixer on low speed, add a quarter the flour mixture to the butter mixture, then add about a quarter of the milk mixture, beating until well combined. Scrape down the sides of the bowl. Repeat, alternating flour and milk and scraping down the bowl until the cake batter is fully mixed.

Use a silicone spatula to fold in 1 cup of rainbow jimmies into the batter so you don't crush the sprinkles.

Divide the batter evenly among the three cake pans. Tap the cake pans gently on the counter to remove air pockets and smooth the tops with a spatula.

Bake for 37 to 40 minutes, or until a toothpick inserted into the center of the cake layers comes out clean.

Let the cakes cool for 20 minutes, then gently flip them onto wire racks and gently remove the pans. Use a thin spatula around the edges to release them if any of the cake sticks. Flip the cake right-side up and let the cake layers cool completely. Gently remove the parchment paper from the cakes once cool.

To decorate: In a large bowl with an electric mixer on medium-high speed, cream the butter and powdered sugar until light and fluffy, about 3 minutes. Add the vanilla and beat until smooth, about 1 minute. Add the cream and whip until thick and creamy, about 3 minutes.

Using a large serrated knife, trim off the rounded top from each cake layer so the layers are flat on both sides. Place a cool cake layer, top-side up, on a large plate. Scoop about a quarter of the frosting onto the cake. Use an icing spatula and spread the frosting evenly on top. Add the second layer, top-side up, on top of the first layer.

Spread the top cake layer with another quarter of the frosting. Top with the third cake layer. Frost and decorate the top and sides with the remaining frosting. Decorate with the sprinkles just after adding the frosting so they stick. Enjoy!

RAINBOW CUPCAKES

Princess Lolly will have everyone stomping their feet and clapping their hands in no time with a song about rainbows to fill any cloudy day with magic. Topped with a fluffy marshmallow frosting cloud and a cheerful rainbow on top, these rainbow cupcakes are colorful and delicious.

YIELD: 24 CUPCAKES

FOR THE CUPCAKES

2¾ cups cake flour

1 tablespoon baking powder

½ teaspoon salt

1 cup (2 sticks) unsalted butter, softened

1¾ cups granulated sugar

4 large eggs

2 large egg yolks

2 teaspoons pure vanilla extract

1 cup sour cream

8 drops blue food coloring

FOR THE FROSTING

½ cup (1 stick) butter, softened

½ cup powdered sugar

One seven-ounce jar marshmallow crème

FOR DECORATING

Rainbow sour belts

Mini marshmallows

To make the cupcakes: In a medium bowl, combine the flour, baking powder, and salt. Set aside.

In a large bowl with an electric mixer on medium speed, cream the butter and granulated sugar until light and fluffy, 3 to 4 minutes. Add the whole eggs and egg yolks, one at a time, beating well after each addition. Turn off the mixer and scrape the sides of the bowl with a silicone spatula. Add the vanilla and mix on medium-high speed until combined.

Add half of the flour mixture and mix on low until just blended. Add the sour cream and food coloring and mix until just combined. Add the remaining flour mixture and mix until just blended.

Preheat the oven to 350°F. Line two 12-cup muffin pans with cupcake liners. Divide the batter evenly among the prepared muffin cups.

Bake for 22 to 24 minutes, until the cupcakes tops are golden brown and a toothpick inserted into the center of a cupcake comes out clean. Let them cool in the pans for 10 minutes, then carefully transfer to wire racks to cool completely.

To make the frosting: In a large bowl with an electric mixer on medium speed, whip the butter until smooth, about 2 minutes. Add the powdered sugar and mix until light and fluffy, 2 to 3 minutes. Add the marshmallow crème and mix until just blended. Using a metal spatula, spread frosting on the tops of the cupcakes.

Halve the sour belts in the short direction and bend to make a rainbow arc. Insert the ends of the sour belts into the frosting on each cupcake to make a rainbow. Arrange mini marshmallows at the base of each arc to look like clouds. Serve and enjoy!

SPARKLE MOUNTAIN CUPCAKES

Swirl a wide frosting base on these magical cupcakes, then work your way to the sparkling top! Queen Frostine calmly and coolly inspects every Sparkle Mountain cupcake herself to make sure it has the perfect fluffy height and just the right amount of shine. Once the cupcakes are ready, Queen Frostine absolutely loves to send these magical sparkling cupcakes topped with shiny sprinkles out into CANDY LAND with a flourish!

YIELD: 12 CUPCAKES

FOR THE CUPCAKES

⅔ cup all-purpose flour

2½ tablespoons unsweetened cocoa powder

¾ teaspoon baking powder

¼ teaspoon salt

11 tablespoons unsalted butter, cut into pieces

3 ounces bittersweet baking chocolate, chopped

¾ cup plus 2 tablespoons granulated sugar

3 large eggs

1 teaspoon pure vanilla extract

Sprinkles for decorating (use a metallic looking sprinkle or bright colored sprinkle to really sparkle and shine on these cupcakes)

FOR THE CHOCOLATE FROSTING

3½ cups powdered sugar

1 cup unsweetened cocoa powder

1 stick unsalted butter, softened

1 teaspoon pure vanilla extract

Pinch salt

1 cup heavy cream

To make the cupcakes: Preheat the oven to 350°F. Line a 12-cup muffin pan with cupcake liners.

In a medium bowl, combine the flour, cocoa powder, baking powder, and salt.

Put the butter and baking chocolate into a microwave-safe bowl. Microwave on high power, stirring every 20 seconds until fully smooth. Let the mixture cool until barely warm, 10 to 15 minutes. Add the granulated sugar to the cooled chocolate mixture and whisk until combined. Add the eggs, one at a time, mixing well after each addition. Add the vanilla and whisk to combine.

Add the flour mixture to the chocolate mixture and mix until just combined. The flour mixture should be fully mixed into the batter but be careful not to overmix.

Divide the batter evenly among the prepared muffin cups.

Bake for 22 to 24 minutes, until a toothpick inserted into the center of a cupcake comes with clean.

Let the cupcakes cool in the pan for 10 minutes, then carefully transfer them to a wire rack to cool completely.

To make the frosting: In a large bowl combine the powdered sugar and cocoa powder. Add the butter. With an electric mixer on low speed, mix the butter just until it looks crumbly. Add the vanilla and salt and mix until combined.

Add the cream to the butter mixture and mix on medium speed for about 1 minute, until smooth and spreadable. If the frosting is too thick, beat in extra cream, 1 tablespoon at a time, until the frosting is smooth and spreadable.

Fit a pastry bag or strong zip-top bag with a medium star tip. Put the bag, tip-end down, in a tall glass and fold back the open end of the bag over the sides of the glass.

Using a spoon, scoop the frosting into the bag to fill, then remove and twist the bag closed.

With your writing hand holding the bag at the twist and your other hand holding it near the tip, pipe the frosting on top of each cupcake in the shape of a mountain.

Put the sprinkles into a small bowl. Gently roll the tops of the cupcakes in sprinkles. Serve and enjoy!

S'MORES CUPCAKES

Duchess E. Claire loves chocolatey delicious s'mores but wanted a way to share the gooiness with King Kandy and Queen Frostine at the Candy Castle. These cupcakes are one of her inventions for portable s'mores, packed with all of that gooey chocolate and sweet marshmallow flavor. She couldn't wait to pack up these cupcakes and share with all her CANDY LAND friends!

YIELD: 12 CUPCAKES

FOR THE CUPCAKES
¾ cup hot water

½ cup unsweetened cocoa powder

1½ teaspoons pure vanilla extract

1¼ cups all-purpose flour

½ teaspoon baking soda

½ teaspoon salt

¾ cup (1½ sticks) unsalted butter, softened

1 cup granulated sugar

2 large eggs, at room temperature

¼ cup semisweet or milk chocolate chips

FOR THE FROSTING
½ cup (1 stick) unsalted butter, softened

½ cup powdered sugar

One seven-ounce jar marshmallow crème

2 graham crackers

To make the cupcakes: Preheat the oven to 350°F. Line a 12-cup muffin pan with cupcake liners.

In a large glass measuring cup, combine the water and cocoa powder, stirring until blended. Add the vanilla and mix again.

In a medium bowl, combine the flour, baking soda, and salt.

In a large bowl with an electric mixer on medium speed, cream the butter and granulated sugar until light and fluffy, about 3 minutes. Add the eggs, one at a time, mixing until just blended after each addition.

Slowly add a third of the flour mixture into the butter mixture and combine. Then add half of the cocoa mixture and combine. Continue alternating the flour and cocoa mixture until the batter is fully combined.

Divide the batter evenly among the prepared muffin cups. Sprinkle the tops of the cupcakes with the chocolate chips. Bake for 17 to 20 minutes, or until a toothpick inserted into the center of a cupcake comes out clean. Allow cupcakes to cool in the pan for 10 minutes, then carefully transfer them to wire racks to cool completely.

To make the frosting: In a large bowl with an electric mixer on medium speed, whip the butter until smooth, about 2 minutes. Add the powdered sugar and mix until light and fluffy, 3 to 4 minutes. Add the marshmallow crème and mix until just blended.

With a metal spatula, spread the frosting on the cupcakes. Place the graham crackers in a strong zip-top bag. Roll over the graham crackers with a rolling pin to make crumbs. Sprinkle the crumbs evenly over the cupcakes, then enjoy!

Fifty percent of all marshmallows sold are sold in the summer, many to toast over a fire and make s'mores.

PB&J CUPCAKES

With both sweet jam and salty peanuts, this delicious combination makes the most magical cupcakes that King Kandy simply cannot resist. Make a big batch of these gooey cupcakes, and everyone will come running! Enjoy these yummy cupcakes with a big glass of creamy ice-cold milk.

YIELD: 12 CUPCAKES

FOR THE CUPCAKES

Nonstick cooking spray or unsalted butter, for greasing

1¼ cups all-purpose flour

1¼ teaspoons baking powder

¼ teaspoon salt

¾ cup granulated sugar

6 tablespoons unsalted butter, softened

2 large eggs

1 teaspoon pure vanilla extract

⅓ cup whole milk

FOR THE FROSTING

6 tablespoons unsalted butter, softened

¾ cup smooth peanut butter

¾ cup powdered sugar, sifted

¼ cup heavy cream

¾ cup fruit jam or preserves

It takes 540 peanuts to make a twelve-ounce jar of peanut butter.

To make the cupcakes: Preheat the oven to 350°F. Generously grease a 12-cup muffin pan with nonstick cooking spray.

In a medium bowl, whisk together the flour, baking powder, and salt. Set aside.

In a large bowl, combine the granulated sugar and butter. With an electric mixer on medium speed, cream until light and fluffy, about 3 minutes. Add the eggs and vanilla and mix until just combined. Scrape down the sides of the bowl with a silicone spatula.

Add half of the flour mixture and mix on low speed until just blended. With the mixer off, add the whole milk then mix on low speed just until combined. With the mixer off, add the rest of the flour mixture, then mix on low speed until fully blended. Scrape down the sides and the bottom of the bowl, making sure all the ingredients are well blended.

Divide the batter evenly among the prepared muffin cups, filling each about three-fourths full. Bake for 18 to 20 minutes, until the cupcake tops are light golden brown and a toothpick inserted into the center comes out clean.

Let cupcakes to cool in the pan for about 10 minutes, then carefully transfer them to wire racks to cool completely.

To make the frosting: In a large bowl, combine the butter, peanut butter, and powdered sugar. With an electric mixer on medium-low speed, mix until smooth and fluffy, 2 to 3 minutes. Add the cream and mix again until smooth.

With a large serrated knife, carefully halve each cupcake horizontally, similar to how you would slice a hamburger bun. Spread about 1 tablespoon of jam on each cupcake bottom, then replace the tops. Using a metal frosting spatula or butter knife, frost the cupcakes. Serve and enjoy!

MINI DOUBLE CHOCOLATE RASPBERRY TARTS

Seeing the Chocolate Falls flow with the sunshine making it extra melty is one of the most majestic views in CANDY LAND. Duchess E. Claire was inspired to make a tart that was just as rich, creamy, and chocolatey! These double chocolate tarts start with a crunchy chocolate bottom, and then are filled with a smooth and creamy chocolate filling. When you take a bite, a surprise burst of raspberry in the center feels just like sunshine!

YIELD: SIX 4-INCH TARTS

FOR THE CRUST
22 chocolate sandwich cookies

5 tablespoons salted butter, melted

FOR THE FILLING
½ cup raspberry preserves, divided

2 tablespoons salted butter, softened

1 cup semisweet chocolate chips

½ cup heavy cream

1 tablespoon granulated sugar

18 raspberries

SPECIALTY TOOLS
6 four-inch tart pans

To make the crust: Preheat the oven to 350°F.

Put the chocolate cookies in a strong zip-top bag, press out the air, and seal shut. Using a rolling pin, roll over the cookies until finely crushed. You can also use a food processor.

In a large bowl, stir together the cookie crumbs and melted butter until the crumbs are no longer dry. Divide the mixture evenly between six 4-inch tart pans. Press firmly with the back of a ¼-cup measure to pack the cookie crust tightly into the pans. Place the tart pans on a rimmed baking sheet.

Bake the cookie crusts for about 7 minutes. Let the crusts cool completely in the pan.

To make the filling: Once the crusts are cool, add 1½ tablespoons of raspberry preserves to the center of each tart crust.

Slice the butter into small six to eight small pieces. In a medium heatproof bowl, combine the chocolate chips and butter.

Put the cream into a microwave-safe bowl. Heat the cream until warm in the microwave, about 1 minute. Pour the cream over the chocolate chips and butter and gently mix with a silicone spatula for about 1 minute. If the chocolate sauce still has lumps, switch to a whisk and stir the chocolate until smooth.

Divide the chocolate mixture evenly among the tart pans, covering the raspberry preserves. Smooth the top of the chocolate with a metal spatula, if needed. Cover the tarts with plastic wrap and refrigerate for at least 2 hours or up to 2 days.

Carefully remove each tart from the pan and place on plates. If needed, use a thin metal spatula to help the tarts release. Top each tart with three fresh raspberries, then enjoy!

BONUS! Sugar and Spice:
These mini tarts can be made in a muffin pan with twelve cups so that each one is half the size of a mini tart. To keep the mini tarts from sticking to the muffin pan, you must place a square of parchment paper in each cup. Then the parchment paper can be used to lift the tarts from the pan. This recipe will stick to standard cupcake liners, so we do not recommend using them for this recipe.

RASPBERRY JELLY ROLL

Princess Lolly has been working on new ways to mix her favorite fruity flavors into CANDY LAND sweets. Princess Lolly couldn't help but sing about this sweet cake when she had the first taste! The result was rich raspberry layers spiraled into a sweet vanilla cake, topped with whipped cream and a delicate layer of powdered sugar that is fruity and fun. Your taste buds are sure to sing along with Princess Lolly!

YIELD: 8 TO 10 SERVINGS

FOR THE CAKE

Unsalted butter, for greasing

⅔ cup cake flour

Pinch salt

4 large eggs, separated

1 large egg yolk

⅔ cup granulated sugar, divided

1 teaspoon pure vanilla extract

Powdered sugar, for dusting

FOR THE SIMPLE SYRUP

¼ cup water

¼ cup granulated sugar

FOR THE FILLING

1 cup heavy cream

1½ cups raspberry jam

To make the cake: Preheat the oven to 350°F.

Generously grease the sides of a 10-by-15-by-1-inch rimmed baking sheet with butter, then line the pan with parchment paper.

In a medium bowl, combine the flour and salt. In a large bowl with an electric mixer on medium speed, beat the 5 egg yolks and ⅓ cup of granulated sugar for 3 minutes, until thickened and pale yellow. Add the vanilla mix until combined. Add the flour mixture to the egg yolk mixture and mix on low for 1 minute, then on medium until the batter forms.

In a separate large bowl with clean beaters, beat the 4 egg whites on medium-high speed until they form soft peaks, 2 to 3 minutes.

With the mixer on medium speed, mix in the remaining ⅓ cup of granulated sugar, a little at a time, and beat until stiff peaks form, 1 to 2 minutes. Be careful not to overmix. If you run a spoon through the mixture, the dent from the spoon should hold its shape.

Using a silicone spatula, fold the egg white mixture, a little at a time, into the batter until just mixed. Carefully spread the batter evenly into the prepared pan.

Bake for 13 to 14 minutes, until the cake is golden brown and a toothpick inserted into the center comes out clean.

While the cake is baking, lay a clean kitchen towel on a clean work surface. Sift powdered sugar all over the towel, covering it evenly and generously so it looks like snow.

Remove the cake from the oven and run a metal spatula or butter knife gently around the inside of the pan to loosen the cake. Holding the pan carefully with oven mitts, flip the pan onto the prepared towel covered in powdered sugar. Lift the pan off the cake and carefully peel off the parchment paper. Quickly before the cake cools, starting with the shorter edge of the cake, gently roll the cake and towel together into a long roll. Let the cake cool completely in the towel.

To make the simple syrup: In a small saucepan over low heat, combine the water and ¼ cup granulated sugar, stirring until the sugar dissolves, 2 to 3 minutes.

To make the filling: In a medium bowl using clean beaters and medium-high speed, beat the cream for about 4 minutes, until medium peaks form and a spoon trailed through the cream holds its shape.

Gently unroll the cooled cake and set the towel aside. Using a silicone brush, add a thin layer of simple syrup to the cake, allowing it to fully soak in. This syrup will help keep the finished cake moist without making it too sweet.

Carefully spread the jam generously and evenly over the cake. Then gently spread the whipped cream generously and evenly over the jam.

Roll up the cake into a long cylinder. Transfer the roll, seam-side down, to a platter. Dust the cake with plenty of powdered sugar. Serve and enjoy!

The thickness of jam comes from pectin, which naturally occurs in fruit, but is brought out by adding sugar and cooking the fruit.

CHAPTER 4
ICE CREAM AND COLD TREATS

■ ■ ■

Ice cream and other cold treats are where Queen Frostine shines brightest! Learn how to dip, whirl, and layer sweet fruit, cream, and other delicious toppings to make tempting cold treats that are cool and refreshing. Queen Frostine encourages you to explore your own creativity with toppings in this chapter, whether it's a drizzle of Homemade Strawberry Sauce **(page 105)** or fun sprinkles, chopped nuts, or candies in every color of the rainbow.

Look for Jubilee Cheesecake Bars **(page 68)** for any special event, Ice Cream Bonbons **(page 64)** that are the perfect bites on a warm day, and the most Cherrific Ice Creamy Floats **(page 71)** you have ever tasted. Packed with dreamy swirls and a sprinkle of fun, the cold treats in this chapter are sure to melt in your mouth.

FROZEN FRUIT POPS

It was a warm day in CANDY LAND when Queen Frostine and Princess Lolly blended together this fruity and cool twisted treat. These frozen fruit pops combine the flavors of mango, pineapple, and strawberry into a magical, breezy treat that's perfect for any hot day. You will need wooden craft sticks and either ice pop molds or paper cups.

YIELD: 4 TO 6 POPS

⅓ cup granulated sugar

⅓ cup water

1 cup frozen or fresh mango pieces

¾ cup fresh orange juice, pineapple juice, or orange-pineapple juice blend, divided

1 cup frozen or fresh pineapple pieces

1 cup frozen or fresh strawberry pieces

In a small saucepan over high heat, combine the granulated sugar and water. Cook, stirring constantly, for 2 to 3 minutes, until the sugar dissolves to form a simple syrup.

Place the mango in a blender. Add ¼ cup of orange juice and 2 tablespoons of simple syrup and blend until smooth. Divide the mango between 6 ice pop molds or 4 paper cups. Freeze for 1 hour.

Rinse the blender. Place the pineapple pieces in the clean blender. Add ¼ cup of orange juice and 2 tablespoons of simple syrup and blend until smooth. Evenly pour the pineapple mixture over the mango in the ice pop molds. Place a wooden craft stick into each mold, then return the ice pops to the freezer for 1 hour.

Rinse the blender and place the strawberries in the clean blender. Add the remaining ¼ cup of orange juice and the remaining syrup. Blend the strawberries until smooth. Pour the strawberry mixture over the pineapple in the ice pop molds. Return the ice pops to the freezer. Freeze for 2 to 4 hours, until firm.

To remove the pops from the molds, dip the bottoms of the molds in a bowl of very hot water until the pops start to loosen, about 20 seconds, then remove and enjoy! Ice pops can be stored in the freezer for 1 week, either in the mold or removed and wrapped in individual bags.

CHOCOLATE-DIPPED STRAWBERRIES

It was the perfect match the day Duchess E. Claire was hiking along the Chocolate Falls, eating some strawberries as a snack. Her berries accidentally fell into the falls, but instead of ruining her snack, it created this amazing treat that she shared with everyone right away. Sweet, creamy chocolate paired with cool, refreshing berries is a berry-rific combination!

YIELD: 4 TO 6 SERVINGS

1 cup semisweet chocolate chips or chopped chocolate

1 tablespoon vegetable shortening

2 pints large strawberries

Chopped nuts or sprinkles (optional)

Chocolate Falls

Place the chocolate chips and the shortening in a small microwave-safe bowl. Melt the chocolate in 20- to 30-second intervals in the microwave, stirring between each one, until the chocolate is smooth, 2 to 3 minutes total.

Line a baking sheet with wax paper or parchment paper. Hold a strawberry by its green stem or leaves. Dip the strawberry into the melted chocolate until it is about three-fourths covered. Use a small spoon, if necessary, to help coat each strawberry with chocolate.

Let the excess chocolate drip back into the bowl. Place each strawberry on the prepared baking sheet. Immediately add nuts or sprinkles (if using), before the chocolate hardens. Repeat for each strawberry.

Refrigerate the covered strawberries for 10 to 15 minutes, or until the chocolate sets. Serve and enjoy!

BONUS! Sugar and Spice:
This treat is best if eaten within 24 hours and must be refrigerated. Try decorating with an extra drizzle of chocolate in a different color to make your treats pop!

FROZEN BANANA STICKS

There is no monkey business here with these sweet frozen banana sticks straight from Duchess E. Claire's creations. Frosty bananas wrapped in luscious chocolate are then topped with colorful sprinkles. Absolutely delicious! Let your creativity shine by adding chopped nuts, coconut, or mini candies to this magical chocolate treat. And don't forget the wooden craft sticks!

YIELD: 6 BANANA STICKS

6 small ripe bananas

Juice of 1 lemon

½ cup semisweet chocolate chips or chopped chocolate

2 teaspoons vegetable shortening

Colorful sprinkles, chopped nuts, or mini candies (optional)

Line a baking sheet with wax paper or parchment paper.

Peel the bananas and chop off the pointed ends. Carefully push a wooden craft stick up the center of each banana. Place the bananas, evenly spaced, on the prepared baking sheet. Using a silicone brush, gently brush the bananas with a little lemon juice to keep the banana from turning brown.

Place the chocolate chips and the shortening in a small microwave-safe bowl. Melt the chocolate in 20- to 30-second intervals in the microwave, stirring between each one, until the chocolate is smooth, 2 to 3 minutes total.

With a spoon, drizzle each banana with chocolate. Add sprinkles immediately (if using), then move to the next banana.

Freeze the bananas for at least 5 hours, then serve and enjoy!

ICE CREAM BONBONS

Cool and creamy on the inside, with a crunchy chocolaty shell on the outside, these bonbons are the perfect frosty bite. They are exactly like the rocky boulders you'll find in the Ice Cream Peaks. Smooth, not jagged, you'll find these boulders adorned with nuts or sprinkles and perched carefully on the Ice Cream Peaks' gentle ridges. Pick one or a few ice cream flavors to wrap in chocolate, then make your own grand boulders with a sweet treat inside—as cool as the mountain air. These ice cream bonbons are one of Queen Frostine's clever ways to make ice cream into a delicious bite-size treat.

YIELD: 20 BONBONS

1 pint ice cream of choice

20 toothpicks

Sprinkles, chopped nuts, or small candies or chocolate, for topping

1½ cups dark chocolate chips or chopped dark chocolate

2 tablespoons vegetable shortening

Line a baking sheet with wax paper or parchment paper. Using a 2-inch cookie scoop, scoop out twenty balls of ice cream and place them on the prepared baking sheet.

Quickly poke a toothpick into each ice cream ball. Freeze until the ice cream is firm, 30 to 60 minutes. Set out several small bowls of your favorite toppings.

Place the chocolate chips and the shortening in a small microwave-safe bowl. Melt the chocolate in 20- to 30-second intervals in the microwave, stirring between each one, until the chocolate is smooth, 2 to 3 minutes total.

Dip the frozen ice cream balls into the melted chocolate, letting the excess drip back into the bowl, then immediately sprinkle the topping ingredients on top. Place each bonbon back on the baking sheet.

Return the pan to the freezer and freeze until the chocolate hardens, about 30 minutes. If desired, the toothpicks may be removed from the bonbons before serving.

Today bonbons are most often a creamy center that is molded or dipped in chocolate, while truffles have a soft chocolate center and are often rolled in cocoa, sprinkles, or nuts.

The word *bonbon* (meaning "good") came from the French royal court and the original word was used for all candy. Now a treat called a bonbon must include 25 percent chocolate, according to French law.

Ice Cream Peaks

ICE CREAM WAFFLE SANDWICHES

Crunchy sweet waffles holding sweet creamy ice cream drizzled with chocolate sauce or caramel make the most amazing sandwich you've ever had. Ice cream waffle sandwiches are the favorite traditional lunch for CANDY LAND hikers enjoying the Ice Cream Peaks. While you can find this delicious cold treat at the top of the Ice Cream Peaks, Queen Frostine is always trying new combinations by adding fruit, sweet fruit sauces, and sprinkles to this delicious delight.

YIELD: 6 TO 12 SANDWICHES

2 pints strawberries, sliced

7 tablespoons granulated sugar, divided

3 large eggs, separated

1½ cups milk

1 tablespoon pure vanilla extract

1 stick unsalted butter, melted

1¾ cups all-purpose flour

2 teaspoons baking powder

¼ teaspoon salt

1 quart ice cream of choice

Gooey Chocolate Sauce (page 95), Buttery Caramel Sauce (page 103), or Homemade Strawberry Sauce (page 105) (optional)

SPECIALTY TOOLS
Waffle iron

In a medium bowl, toss together the strawberries and 4 tablespoons of granulated sugar. Set aside but stir occasionally until the berries soften and become syrupy, 30 to 45 minutes.

Preheat a waffle iron. In a medium bowl with an electric mixer on medium-high speed, whip the three egg whites until soft peaks form, about 3 minutes. Add the remaining 3 tablespoons of granulated sugar and whip until stiff peaks form and hold their shape easily, 2 to 3 minutes.

In a sauce pot over medium heat, heat the milk until it is warm to the touch. Transfer the warm milk to a medium bowl, then add the vanilla. Slowly whisk in the three egg yolks and the butter.

In a large bowl, combine the flour, baking powder, and salt. Make a well in the center of the flour mixture and pour in the milk mixture. Stir until a batter just forms. Gently fold the egg white mixture into the batter.

Using a ⅓- to ½-cup measure, pour the batter into the waffle iron. (Follow your model's instructions. For example, if you have a Belgian waffle iron, you may need ¾ cup of batter per waffle.)

Spread the batter starting in the center so that it almost reaches the edges of the hot waffle iron. Cook for 3 to 4 minutes, until the waffle is crisp and brown. Carefully remove the waffle from the waffle iron and repeat with the remaining batter. Cool completely on a wire rack so they stay crisper on the outside.

Allow the ice cream to soften on the counter for about 10 minutes. Separate the waffles into quarters or halves, depending on the size of your waffles. Scoop the ice cream onto half of the pieces.

Drizzle 1 to 2 tablespoons of chocolate sauce (if using) on top of the ice cream in each sandwich. Top with the other waffle. Wrap each sandwich in plastic wrap and freeze for 30 to 60 minutes, then remove and enjoy. The ice cream often will become very soft so a little extra time in the freezer makes this dish even more delicious (and less messy).

It takes three gallons of milk to make one gallon of ice cream.

The largest ice cream cone was ten feet high and made in Norway in 2015.

JUBILEE
CHEESECAKE BARS

Creamy, dreamy cheesecake with a big splash of colorful sprinkles all on a buttery graham cracker crust? Delicious! When Queen Frostine has a larger group of friends over to Candy Castle, these magical Jubilee Cheesecake Bars are the cutest treat at her party to share. Top with whipped cream and sprinkles right before eating for the last touch!

YIELD: 32 BARS

FOR THE CRUST

19 graham crackers

2 tablespoons granulated sugar

¾ teaspoon ground cinnamon

1 stick unsalted butter, melted

FOR THE FILLING

4 large eggs, at room temperature

24 ounces cream cheese (3 sticks), softened

1 cup granulated sugar

2 teaspoons pure vanilla extract

3 tablespoons all-purpose flour

½ cup sour cream

1 cups rainbow jimmie sprinkles, divided

Dreamy Whipped Cream (page 99)

To make the crust: Preheat the oven to 325°F. Press a 20-inch piece of aluminum foil into the bottom and over the sides of a 13-by-9-by-2-inch baking pan.

Place the graham crackers in a strong gallon-size zip-top bag. Roll over them gently with a rolling pin until they become crumbs (or use a food processor). You should have about 2¾ cups of crumbs.

In a medium bowl, combine the graham cracker crumbs, 2 tablespoons of granulated sugar, and cinnamon. Add the butter and stir until the crumbs are no longer dry. Press the crumb mixture into the bottom of the pan. Use a large measuring cup to pack the crumbs in tightly. Bake for about 10 minutes. Remove from the oven and let the crust cool completely.

To make the filling: In a medium bowl using a whisk or fork, whisk together the eggs, then set aside. In a large bowl with an electric mixer on medium speed, combine the cream cheese, 1 cup granulated sugar, and vanilla for 1 to 2 minutes, until it's smooth with no lumps. Scrape down the sides of the bowl with a silicone spatula.

Add the flour to the cream cheese mixture and combine on medium speed for about 1 minute. Scrape down the sides and the bottom of the bowl with a silicone spatula frequently to fully mix the cheesecake filling. Add about half the eggs and

continue mixing until smooth. Add the other half of the eggs and mix until smooth, 1 to 2 minutes. Add the sour cream and beat just until just mixed in, about 30 seconds.

With a silicone spatula, gently fold ¾ cup of rainbow jimmies into the cream cheese filling. Pour the filling into the crust and top with remaining ¼ cup of jimmies.

Bake for 40 to 45 minutes, until the filling has set in the middle of the cheesecake. Give the pan a gentle shake to see if the filling is set and does not wobble in the middle. Allow the pan to cool completely, about 1 hour, then refrigerate for at least 4 hours, until firm, or overnight.

Lift the cheesecake out of the pan onto a cutting surface. Warm a sharp knife under hot water, then slice the cheesecake into quarters, and then each quarter into eight equal pieces. Carefully wipe the blade with a towel between cuts and rewarm the blade with more hot water as needed. This helps keep the cuts straight and clean.

Top with a dollop of whipped cream and a few more sprinkles right before serving. Enjoy!

Cream cheese was an American addition to cheesecake and was first created by a US dairy farmer who was trying to replicate the creamy French cheese Neufchâtel.

CHERRIFIC
ICE CREAM FLOATS

Cherry-pick the best party drink straight from the springs of Queen Frostine's Ice Cream Peaks! Twist and whirl together black cherry soda with creamy cherry chocolate chip ice cream, then top it with a chocolate drizzle. You've never had an ice cream float like this!

YIELD: 2 FLOATS

2 scoops cherry chocolate chip ice cream

12 ounces black cherry soda or cream soda

Dreamy Whipped Cream (page 99) (optional)

Gooey Chocolate Sauce (page 95) (optional)

2 maraschino cherries (optional)

Thomas Jefferson was believed to have written down the first recipe for ice cream, and it was vanilla.

Prepare two 8-ounce drinking glasses. Place a scoop of cherry chocolate chip ice cream in each glass.

Carefully and slowly pour the black cherry soda over the ice cream, splitting it equally between the two glasses. If no black cherry soda is available, cream soda is also delicious.

Top with whipped cream, a drizzle of chocolate syrup, and a maraschino cherry (if using). Add a straw and enjoy!

SWEET STRAWBERRY PUDDING

Sweet strawberry drizzled into pudding is so berry nice! When Princess Lolly first had a taste of this dreamy treat, she broke into song, knowing this fruity pudding was totally her jam. You will love this creamy pudding at first bite, too!

YIELD: 4 TO 6 PUDDING CUPS

¼ cup water, warm

3 teaspoons unsweetened unflavored powdered gelatin

1 cup whole milk

¾ cup powdered sugar

2 teaspoons pure vanilla extract

2½ cups buttermilk

2 cups small diced strawberries, divided

Dreamy Whipped Cream (page 99) (optional)

Pour the water into a small bowl. Sprinkle the gelatin powder into the water and stir well. Let the gelatin stand for 5 minutes to soften.

In a saucepan over medium heat, stir together the whole milk, powdered sugar, and vanilla until it boils. Immediately turn down the heat to medium-low and simmer for 5 minutes.

Add the gelatin mixture to the pot and stir until dissolved. Remove the pot from the heat until cool to the touch, about five minutes.

Add the buttermilk and 1 cup of strawberries to the milk mixture. Stir everything together until combined.

Divide the pudding evenly among four to six small glasses. Cover and refrigerate the glasses with plastic wrap and rubber bands. Store the remaining 1 cup of strawberries in an airtight container in the refrigerator. Chill the pudding for at least 3 hours or overnight.

Before serving, add the fresh strawberries to the top of the pudding. Add whipped cream (if using). Serve cold and enjoy!

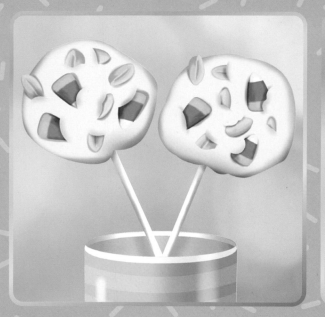

CHAPTER 5
CANDY-BASED AND BAKE-FREE TREATS

■ ■ ■

When in CANDY LAND, let's make candy. Candy-making is King Kandy's favorite pastime. Here we can make all kinds of new candy creations to try and love. Make different kinds of lollipops, learn how to make gummy candy sweet and sour, or mix up a custom batch of trail mix that has all of your favorite treats.

Sculpt, sprinkle, and dip with treats, such as Sour Gummy Bear Scepters (**page 77**), sweet and gooey Ultimate Caramel Apple Lollipops (**page 84**), and Double Minty White Chocolate Bark (**page 86**) that swirls together lots of peppermint candies! You'll love all of the fun candy and no-bake treats in here.

SOUR GUMMY BEAR SCEPTERS

Magically turn regular gummy bears into sweet and sour gummy bear scepters fit for King Kandy with this recipe! While King Kandy certainly loves these sweet glittery gummy bear candy scepters, it's Jolly who can't help but nibble on these portable sweet and sour treats. You'll find him spending his days hiking through the Gumdrop Mountains, adding more gummy treats to his sweet snack and cracking jokes. Now you can make treats just like Jolly does.

YIELD: 6 TO 7 SKEWERS

3 ounces sweetened gelatin mix of choice

4 ounces gummy bear candies or other plain gummy candies

1 to 2 tablespoons lime juice

6 to 7 bamboo skewers

The world's largest gumdrop was over ten pounds!

Gummy bears were originally known as Dancing Bears.

Line a rimmed baking sheet with parchment paper or wax paper. Pour the gelatin dessert mix onto a second rimmed baking sheet, keeping it in a small pile. Place five to six gummy bears onto the ends of bamboo skewers.

With a silicone brush, brush the gummy bears on the skewers with the lime juice. Roll the gummy bears in the powdered gelatin mix. Place the finished wands onto the prepared baking sheet. Repeat with the remaining gummy bears.

Enjoy immediately or store the gummy bears in an airtight container on the counter. If there are any spots on the candy that are damp, refrigerate for 20 minutes to help them finish drying before storing.

BONUS! Sugar and Spice:
Try experimenting with different shapes of gummies and different flavors of gelatin mix. (We especially liked raspberry!) You can make colorful candy skewers to match any party theme or for any holiday.

NUTTY CANDY CORN WHITE CHOCOLATE LOLLIPOPS

Creamy, sweet, and just the right amount of salty, these white chocolate lollipops are amazingly delicious! While Princess Lolly knows it may be a little corny, she is *nuts* about these unique lollipops. Smooth white chocolate pairs perfectly with crunchy, salty peanuts and candy corn, which is sweet like vanilla and honey mixed together. Soon you'll be singing from the rooftops about these fun lollipops!

YIELD: 12 LOLLIPOPS

¼ cup salted roasted peanuts

¼ cup candy corn

10 to 12 ounces (about 1½ cups) white chocolate chips

1 tablespoon shortening, coconut oil, or vegetable oil

SPECIALTY TOOLS
12 lollipop sticks

White chocolate technically does not contain chocolate solids but rather cocoa butter, which is made from chocolate.

Place two pieces of parchment paper on two flat baking sheets or a cutting board with parchment paper. Place a freezer zip-top bag into a tall drinking glass with a corner down into the glass. Fold the zip-top part over the edges of the glass, opening the bag.

Roughly chop the peanuts. Transfer to a small bowl, then place the candy corn in a second small bowl. Place the bowl near the parchment paper, then place lollipop sticks nearby.

In a large microwave-safe bowl, combine the white chocolate chips and shortening. Heat in the microwave at half power for 1 minute. Stir the white chocolate with a clean dry spoon, then heat for an additional 30 seconds. Continue heating, 30 seconds at a time, and stirring until the white chocolate has completely melted and is smooth. Be careful not to get any liquid in the white chocolate or it could seize and become grainy.

Pour the melted white chocolate into the zip-top bag in the glass. Close the bag, gently pushing the chocolate down to one corner.

Take the chocolate to the parchment paper. Carefully snip a hole in the corner of the bag that is about a ¼ inch wide with the corner turned up (the chocolate will be a bit drippy and will come out of the bag quickly). Use the bag to make 2½-inch-diameter circles of white chocolate on the parchment paper.

Quickly press a lollipop stick into each circle of white chocolate, twisting it so both sides of the stick sink into the white chocolate.

Quickly sprinkle each lollipop with chopped nuts. Press three to four pieces of candy corn into each lollipop. Let the lollipops cool for at least 15 minutes. Refrigerate or freeze to help the chocolate set faster. Once the chocolate hardens, the lollipops are ready to enjoy!

BONUS! Sugar and Spice:
Mini caramel bites or chopped toffee bits (with or without chocolate on them) are also delicious additions to these lollipops! A spoon can also be used to form the melted chocolate into lollipops, but it's much less messy to use a bag!

RICE CRISPY WANDS

Standing over the entire land is a big responsibility, but Queen Frostine stands with beauty, grace, and a colorful magic wand to help her! Make your own colorful wands out of a sweet marshmallow cereal treat. These wands can be made even more magical by tying colorful ribbons onto the handles and sprinkling colorful mini candies on top! You will need wooden craft sticks and a 3½-inch shaped cookie cutter, such as a star, heart, or circle!

YIELD: 12 POPS

3 tablespoons salted butter

4 cups mini marshmallows

6 cups crispy rice cereal, divided

All-purpose flour, for dusting

Two 12-ounce bags candy melts in two colors

2 tablespoons vegetable shortening, divided

Colorful mini candies or sprinkles, for decorating

Line a 9-by-13-inch baking pan and a rimmed baking sheet with parchment paper. Cut two extra pieces of parchment paper that fit over the 9-by-13-inch pan.

Place the butter in a large saucepan with high sides. Place over low heat and melt the butter. Add the marshmallows, stirring until they just lose their shape, about 1 minute.

Add 3 cups of cereal and stir gently until mixed. Be careful when mixing not to crush the cereal. Add the remaining 3 cups of cereal and stir gently until fully mixed.

Transfer the cereal mixture to the prepared pan. Lay a sheet of parchment on top of the cereal. Gently press the cereal into the pan but not so hard it breaks the cereal. Refrigerate for 30 minutes to cool.

Lift the cereal bars out of the pan with the parchment paper. Dust a 3½-inch cookie cutter with flour. Cut shapes from the cereal mixture as closely together as possible. Dust the cookie cutter with more flour if it starts to stick. Any scraps can be pushed into the cookie cutter to make one final shape.

Combine one color of candy melts and 1 tablespoon of vegetable shortening in a medium microwave-safe bowl. Microwave for 1 minute at half power, then stir. Continue to microwave, 30 seconds at a time, stirring between each interval, until the candy melts and is smooth.

Pour the mini candies into a small bowl. With a spoon in one hand and a fork in the other hand, carefully dip each cereal treat into the melted candy melts. The spoon can help to finish covering the crispy treat, and you can let the excess candy melts drip through the fork as you remove the treat. Tap away any extra melted candy through the fork, then place on the remaining piece of parchment. Immediately add sprinkles or mini colorful candies on top of the warm chocolate. Add a wooden craft stick and sprinkles quickly after coating in candy melts.

Melt the other color of candy melts when the first bowl is empty. Repeat the process of dipping cereal treats with the remaining ingredients.

Slide the cereal treats on parchment paper onto baking sheets. Refrigerate the treats for at least 20 minutes or until the candy sets before serving. You can tie ribbons onto the wooden sticks to make them even more magical. The wands can be stored in an airtight container for about three days.

Ancient Egyptians were the first to enjoy marshmallows. The sweet was used for coughs and sore throats but was typically for royalty and gods only.

SPRINKLE STRAWBERRY BROWNIE CONES

These delicious brownie cones are always available at Candy Castle, earning King Kandy major *brownie* points with all his friends. To make your own, start by coating a waffle cone in chocolate and sprinkles, add brownie pieces and fresh strawberries, and top it off with some whipped cream. Then enjoy a decadent handheld treat that is super easy to share, or get creative and add your favorite toppings! Try dipping the cones ahead of time and then letting your guests pick their favorite toppings. You'll surely earn some brownie points with them!

YIELD: 10 CONES

½ cup sprinkles

10 to 12 ounces chocolate chips

1 tablespoon shortening, coconut oil, or vegetable oil

10 waffle cones

Premade brownies (store-bought or boxed mix)

1 pint strawberries

Dreamy Whipped Cream (page 99)

The very first ice cream cone was created in Italy. Ice cream was sold as street food in all different shapes of bowls. The cone helped street vendors avoid breaking bowls and spoons, but the cones were not eaten and were more for sanitation.

Line a baking sheet with parchment paper. Place the sprinkles in a medium bowl wide enough that the top of the waffle cones will fit inside.

Combine the chocolate chips and the shortening in a medium microwave-safe bowl wide enough that the top of the waffle cones will fit inside. Heat in the microwave at half power for 1 minute. Stir the chocolate then place it back in the microwave at half power for 30 seconds. Continue to microwave, 30 seconds at a time, stirring between each interval, until the chocolate is melted and smooth.

Dip the top of a waffle cone into the chocolate then immediately dip it in the sprinkles. Place the waffle cone on its side on the parchment paper. Repeat for all waffle cones. Refrigerate to help set the chocolate.

Slice the brownies into bite-size pieces. Slice the strawberries into pieces, removing the stems.

Right before serving, fill the cones with brownies and strawberries. Top with whipped cream and enjoy!

BONUS! Sugar and Spice:
This idea also works great as a build-your-own-style treat for a party where everyone can add their favorite fruit, chocolate, whipped cream, or even more sprinkles.

ULTIMATE CARAMEL APPLE LOLLIPOPS

When apple-flavored lollipops started sprouting on Lollipop Lane, Princess Lolly had the perfect idea! Coating the lollipops in warm caramel and peanuts made a delicious treat. But she didn't stop there, sprinkling her gooey caramel creations with sprinkles, mini chocolate chips, rainbow chocolate candies, and pecans for the ultimate lollipops!

YIELD: 6 LOLLIPOPS

30 to 36 green apple candies (such as Jolly Ranchers)

¼ cup plus 2 tablespoons roasted salted peanuts (or your favorite caramel apple toppings)

24 wrapped soft caramels

2 tablespoons heavy cream or half-and-half

SPECIALTY TOOLS
6 lollipop sticks

Preheat the oven to 250°F. Line a rimmed baking sheet with parchment paper.

Unwrap the green apple candies. Lay the candies on the prepared baking sheet in rows of five to six candies with the longer sides of the candy touching to form tall rectangles. Each row of five to six candies will make its own tall lollipop. Leave at least two inches of space between each lollipop on the pan.

Carefully place the baking sheet of candies into the oven, being careful not to let the candies roll on the pan. Move the candies back into rectangle shapes with the long side of the candies touching if needed before they go into the oven for each lollipop.

Bake for 7 to 9 minutes, until the candies fully melt and have lost their shape.

Remove the candies from the oven and carefully slide the parchment paper off the pan and onto the counter. Immediately add lollipop sticks to each lollipop, placing at least 1½ inches of the stick into the melted candy. Give the stick a twist so the green candy covers the top of the stick in the lollipop. Let the lollipops cool on the parchment paper for at least 10 minutes.

Roughly chop the peanuts.

Unwrap the caramels and place them in a medium microwave-safe bowl with the heavy cream. Microwave for 1 minute, then stir. Microwave for 30 seconds at a time, stirring between each interval, until a smooth sauce forms.

Drizzle the caramel over top of the lollipops while they are on the parchment paper. Don't worry if some of the caramel goes over the edges of the candy. Immediately sprinkle the chopped nuts on the caramel while it's still warm. Refrigerate the lollipops for at least 10 minutes.

Peel the caramel apple lollipops from the parchment paper. Any excess caramel can be wrapped around the back of the lollipop. Eat and enjoy! Store lollipops in an airtight container with layers of parchment paper between them.

DOUBLE MINTY WHITE CHOCOLATE BARK

Mayor Mint loves every part of the Peppermint Forest, but one day he realized his sweet candy cane trees had no bark! He created this double minty white chocolate bark in honor of the Peppermint Forest. This bark is packed full of peppermint flavor that comes straight from the candy cane trees, and the white chocolate reminds Mayor Mint of the fresh fallen snow that's found in the frosty Peppermint Forest. Everyone can enjoy a small (or large!) piece of Mayor Mint's favorite sweet place in CANDY LAND.

YIELD: 10 SERVINGS

16 round peppermint hard candies

½ cup chocolate mint candy, such as Andes mints or mint M&M's, chopped

½ cup mini marshmallows

10 to 12 ounces white chocolate chips

½ cup red candy melts

1 tablespoon shortening, coconut oil, or vegetable oil

Line a rimmed baking sheet with a large piece of parchment paper. Crush the peppermint candies in a zip-top bag with a rolling pin. Transfer the crushed peppermint, chocolate mint candy, and marshmallows to three separate small bowls next to the baking sheet.

Place the white chocolate chips and the shortening in a small microwave-safe bowl. Put the candy melts in separate small microwave-safe bowl. Add a piece of parchment paper with two spoons close to the microwave.

Microwave the white chocolate chips for 1 minute at half power, then stir with one of the spoons. Continue to microwave 30 seconds at a time, stirring between each interval, until the white chocolate chips are melted and smooth.

Microwave the red candy melts for 1 minute at half power, then stir with the other spoon. Continue to microwave 30 seconds at a time, stirring between each interval, until the candy melts are melted and smooth.

Put the white chocolate back in the microwave for 30 seconds, then stir so it stays a liquid.

Pour the white chocolate onto the parchment paper and smooth with a metal spatula or butter knife.

Starting at the top of the parchment paper, pour a stripe of red-colored candy melts back and forth acros the white chocolate the short direction. Move down the white chocolate making wide red stripe drizzles.

Take a butter knife and run it through the chocolate the long direction making red swirls in the chocolate.

Top the chocolate bark with the crushed peppermint, chocolate mint candies, and marshmallows. Freeze the bark until the chocolate fully sets, then slice with a knife or break apart into chunks and enjoy.

The first white chocolate bar debuted in 1936 in Switzerland.

Real white chocolate is slightly yellow in color, not white, because the cocoa butter is ivory colored.

JOLLY'S EASY PARTY TRAIL MIX

Jolly loves a sweet and salty trail mix, but he never makes the same mix twice! You, too, can make your own custom mix. Just grab a big bowl and some of your favorite snacks to make a delicious sweet and salty mix! For the best mix, add at least one sweet and one crunchy salty item, but you can totally get creative to make your favorite blend. There's no wrong way to make Jolly's Easy Party Trail Mix!

SWEET IDEAS

- Caramel corn
- Chocolate chips
- Chocolate-covered nuts
- Colorful chocolate candies
- Dried cranberries
- Mini graham crackers
- Mini marshmallows
- Peanut butter candies
- Peanut butter chips
- Raisins

CRUNCHY SALTY IDEAS

- Almonds
- Cereal
- Cheese crackers
- Peanuts
- Large cereal, such as Chex
- Pecans
- Popcorn
- Pretzels

Peanut butter cups have been made into many shapes, including trees, bells, eggs, hearts, bunnies, ghosts, and snowmen.

Marshmallows were originally made from the root of the mallow plant. Now, egg whites and cornstarch are whipped together with sugar and water to make the spongy sweets we know and love.

CHAPTER 6
TOPPINGS AND DRINKS

■ ■ ■

Give a little pinch of sprinkles or a drizzle of sweet sauce for an extra splash of fun! Here you'll find some of Queen Frostine's favorite ways to add an extra special drop of deliciousness to ice cream, cupcakes, and waffles. You'll also find some delightful drinks to sip, which are the perfect way to add a little extra sparkle to your glass.

Try making Gooey Chocolate Sauce (**page 95**), colorful Homemade Sprinkles (**page 96**), or a sweet spoonful of Homemade Strawberry Sauce (**page 105**)! Wash it down with a cool glass of Candy Pop Punch (**page 109**) or a warm glass of Minty Hot Cocoa (**page 106**).

MARSHMALLOW CREAM TOPPING

Fluffy dreamy marshmallow cream makes the softest peaks—and the sweetest topping. Queen Frostine loves to use this marshmallow cream on top of ice cream, to swirl between two cookies, or to top a mug of Minty Hot Cocoa (page 106)! Dip graham crackers, cookies, or fruit in this marshmallow topping. Or try it in Ice Cream Waffle Sandwiches (page 66), yum!

YIELD: 10 SERVINGS

2 large egg whites

1 cup mini marshmallows

1 cup granulated sugar

¼ cup light corn syrup

½ teaspoon cream of tartar

Pinch salt

6 tablespoons water

1 teaspoon pure vanilla extract

> Marshmallows come in lots of shapes, colors, and flavors, such as peppermint, peanut butter, pumpkin spice, strawberry, mixed fruit, sugar cookie, and chocolate stuffed. You can also find colorful shaped cereal marshmallows, unicorn marshmallows, bunny marshmallows, giant campfire marshmallows, and mini marshmallows.

Find a large heatproof bowl that fits snuggly on top of a medium saucepan (do not use a plastic bowl; it will melt). Place the saucepan over medium-high heat with about 1 to 1½ inches of water in the bottom. Bring to a boil, then lower the heat to medium-low so the water is at a simmer.

In the heatproof bowl, combine the egg whites, marshmallows, granulated sugar, corn syrup, cream of tartar, salt, and water. Place the bowl on top of the saucepan so that it rests but is not touching the water. If the water touches the bowl, remove some of the water.

With a metal whisk, stir the mixture until the granulated sugar and marshmallows have dissolved, about 3 minutes. The mixture is very warm to the touch so be careful and use oven mitts. Remove the bowl from the saucepan and place on a trivet or kitchen towel folded over several times.

With an electric mixer on medium-high speed, carefully whip the marshmallow mixture for about 2 minutes, until soft peaks begin to form that resemble mountains. Shut off the mixer and add the vanilla. Turn the mixer speed on low and mix the vanilla in. Use right away and enjoy!

GOOEY CHOCOLATE SAUCE

Smooth and rich, this chocolate sauce comes straight from the most majestic spot at the Chocolate Falls, where the chocolate cascades down in waves. Make this delicious chocolate sauce to drizzle on sweet drinks, fruit, or Ice Cream Waffle Sandwiches (**page 66**)! Serve the sauce warm over ice cream, with chunks of fruit to dip, or over the Sprinkle Magic Silver Dollar Pancakes (**page 19**).

YIELD: 8 SERVINGS

1 cup semisweet chocolate chips

2 tablespoons light corn syrup or maple syrup

1¼ cups heavy cream

In a small heatproof bowl, combine the chocolate chips and corn syrup.

Pour the cream into a small saucepan and place it over medium heat. Warm the cream until it just starts to simmer.

Pour the hot cream over the chocolate chips. Start mixing gently, first with a silicone spatula and then with a whisk as the chocolate melts, blending until smooth.

Serve warm or make ahead and reheat gently over low heat. You can also let the chocolate come to room temperature on the counter before serving. Don't reheat this sauce on high heat, though! If the chocolate gets too hot, it will separate and become grainy.

The first candy chocolate bar was invented in 1847 by Joseph Fry, who was trying to make chocolate drinking tabs to make hot chocolate. Before that, chocolate was mostly consumed by drinking it from a glass. Fry had been trying to make portioned tabs of chocolate for drinking but discovered people enjoyed eating chocolate as much as drinking it.

HOMEMADE SPRINKLES

Sprinkles can be the sweet, colorful finish on almost any treat. King Kandy makes sure the sprinkle supply in CANDY LAND is always full with every color of the rainbow. These sprinkles are made of royal icing which is the same frosting used to decorate cookies like Gingerbread Movers Cookies (**page 36**). Once the frosting is piped into thin rods and allowed to dry, it can make all kinds of treats pop! Try adding them to the top of the Sweet Strawberry Jam Toaster Tarts (**page 13**).

YIELD: ½ CUP

2 cups powdered sugar

1½ tablespoons meringue powder

3 tablespoons warm water

¼ teaspoon pure vanilla extract

Food coloring, preferably gel type

Line two baking sheets with parchment or wax paper.

In a large bowl, combine the powdered sugar, meringue powder, warm water, and vanilla. With an electric mixer on medium speed, mix for 7 to 8 minutes, until fluffy yet still a little dense.

Divide the icing into three or four small bowls, one for each color you plan to make. Add food coloring to each bowl, stirring well with a spoon until mixed. Add food coloring a little bit at a time until you get the right color. If using liquid food coloring, the colors won't be as bright.

Test to make sure the icing is the right consistency, which can vary depending on how much food coloring you have added to the sprinkles. Scoop up a spoonful and drizzle it into the bowl. The icing should easily form a thin ribbon on top of the icing in the bowl.

If the icing is too thick, add warm water, ¼ teaspoon at a time. If the icing is too runny, add powdered sugar, 1 teaspoon at a time, until it thickens.

Spoon the icing into a pastry bag fitted with a ⅛-inch plain tip. You can also use a strong zip-top bag and cut a tiny hole from the corner, but the sprinkles will not be the exact same thickness like it will be if you use a pastry bag with a frosting tip.

Pipe the icing in straight lines onto the prepared baking sheets. Let the icing dry on the pans for about 24 hours.

Roll the dried sprinkle strands with clean dry fingers to break them up. You can also use a knife to cut them into pieces. These homemade sprinkles are best when used as a decoration on top of treats rather than baked into the treats themselves.

BONUS! Sugar and Spice:
This recipe can also be used as a frosting for the Gingerbread Movers Cookies (page 36). Prepare the recipe as directed and place the mixture in a piping bag. Instead of making it into thin lines, use it to decorate the cookies!

DREAMY WHIPPED CREAM

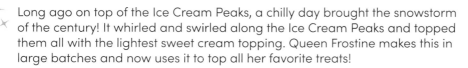

Long ago on top of the Ice Cream Peaks, a chilly day brought the snowstorm of the century! It whirled and swirled along the Ice Cream Peaks and topped them all with the lightest sweet cream topping. Queen Frostine makes this in large batches and now uses it to top all her favorite treats!

YIELD: 2 CUPS

1 cup heavy cream, cold

1½ tablespoons granulated sugar

½ teaspoon pure vanilla extract

After the trend of being sold in cones, ice cream was pressed into molds, frozen, and wrapped in paper. This was called a hokey pokey!

In a large bowl, combine the cream, granulated sugar, and vanilla. With an electric mixer on medium-high speed, whip for 6 to 7 minutes, until soft peaks that look like mountains form and a spoon moves easily through the soft whipped cream. Be careful not to step away from the mixer, as overwhipping can cause the mixture to break and butter to form!

Enjoy right away or cover and refrigerate for 1 to 2 days.

BONUS! Sugar and Spice:
Make a lemon variation: Mix equal parts Sweet Sunshine Lemon Curd (page 101) and whipped cream, whipping with an electric mixer until soft and pillowy, for a light, lemony filling, waffle topping, or ice cream topping.

SWEET SUNSHINE LEMON CURD

King Kandy one day asked Princess Lolly to make him a pitcher of lemonade. She put the ingredients in a big pot and started heating it like she would to make a sweet lollipop! Her lemonade didn't seem quite right while she was mixing it, but this delicious lemon curd became the happy accident. King Kandy was so pleased at the new creation that for weeks he used this sweet lemon curd on top of every treat! Lemon curd can be spread on toast, added to pancakes or waffles, or used to top vanilla ice cream. See the Dreamy Whipped Cream directions on **page 99** to make lemon whipped cream.

YIELD: 1 CUP

1 teaspoon finely grated lemon zest

6 tablespoons fresh lemon juice (about 2 large lemons or 3 small lemons)

3 tablespoons fresh orange juice

2 large eggs, at room temperature

⅓ cup granulated sugar

2 tablespoons unsalted butter

2 tablespoons heavy cream

In a small saucepan, combine the lemon zest, lemon juice, orange juice, eggs, granulated sugar, butter, and cream. Use a whisk to blend everything well.

Place the saucepan over medium-high heat. Cook, whisking constantly, until the curd is smooth and thick, 4 to 5 minutes. It should have the consistency of warm jam. Watch the curd carefully and do not overcook. If not stirred constantly or if overcooked, lumps will begin to form. If you start to see any lumps remove the curd from the heat immediately. If you have just a few lumps they can easily be removed with a spoon.

Pour the lemon curd into a small bowl and cover with plastic wrap. Press the plastic wrap directly onto the surface to keep a skin from forming. Let the bowl cool, then refrigerate until needed.

If your curd is too thick when it's time to use, mix in extra orange juice, 1 to 2 teaspoons at a time, until it is at the right consistency.

BUTTERY CARAMEL SAUCE

If you listen carefully, you may hear the sound of a softly bubbling creek near the Ice Cream Peaks. This creek is in a secret location that only Queen Frostine knows about. She makes the trip to the creek often to scoop up the sweet caramel for all of the CANDY LAND desserts. You can make some of her sweet, magical caramel, too, with only a few ingredients.

YIELD: 1⅓ CUPS

14 ounces soft caramels

¼ cup evaporated milk

2 tablespoons unsalted butter

Place the caramels and evaporated milk in a small saucepan, then place over medium-high heat. Cook, stirring frequently, for 4 to 5 minutes, or until melted and smooth.

Add the butter and stir well until melted and combined.

Use immediately or allow to cool, then cover. Store in an airtight container in the refrigerator for up to 1 week. This caramel sauce can be gently reheated to serve warm or be used chilled.

The two main ingredients in caramel are sugar and milk. Sometimes heavy cream and butter are used in place of milk. The dairy is what makes the caramel creamy.

HOMEMADE STRAWBERRY SAUCE

Sweet strawberry sauce is the most berry special topping in CANDY LAND! This slightly sticky sweet sauce adds a burst of magic and strawberry flavor to any dessert. Try adding it on top of the Jubilee Cheesecake Bars (page 68) right before serving. Jolly is a big fan!

YIELD: 1 CUP

1 pint strawberries, sliced

½ cup granulated sugar

2 tablespoons fresh orange juice

2 tablespoons fresh lemon juice

Combine the strawberries, granulated sugar, orange juice, and lemon juice in a medium saucepan over medium-low heat. Cook, stirring occasionally, for about 6 minutes, until the strawberries break down and the sauce becomes syrupy and thickened.

Puree the sauce with an immersion blender right in the pot if you have one. If using a regular blender or food processor, allow the sauce to cool at least 5 to 10 minutes before blending.

Enjoy the strawberry sauce warm or cold. Store in an airtight container in the refrigerator for several days.

MINTY HOT COCOA

Mayor Mint was so excited when he created this minty hot cocoa, which is rich and chocolaty with just the right amount of peppermint sweetness. It's an amazing warm drink perfect for sharing, especially on a chilly day. Pure magic! Pick a mug and your favorite toppings for a rich, bubbly, chocolaty peppermint treat you'll surely love.

YIELD: 8 SERVINGS

8 cups milk, divided

¼ cup unsweetened cocoa powder

¼ cup granulated sugar

1 teaspoon peppermint extract (essence, not oil)

Mini marshmallows, Dreamy Whipped Cream (see page 99), crushed peppermint, or your favorite toppings (optional)

Ancient Greeks thought peppermint could cure hiccups.

Fine chocolate officially has four categories: white chocolate, milk chocolate, dark chocolate, and unsweetened chocolate.

In a medium saucepan over medium heat, warm the milk until it just begins to simmer and small bubbles appear around the edges of the pan. Turn the heat to low.

In a medium heat-proof bowl, combine the cocoa powder and granulated sugar. Add ¼ cup of warm milk into the cocoa powder mixture, whisking until the powder is well blended without any lumps. Add the peppermint extract and keep mixing until well blended.

Just before serving, heat the remaining milk over medium heat until it again begins to gently simmer. Stir the chocolate mixture into the warm milk with a whisk. Once the cocoa is fully mixed, reduce the heat to low. Divide the cocoa evenly among eight mugs.

Garnish each warm mug of hot cocoa with a sprinkle of mini marshmallows (if using), then enjoy!

BONUS! Sugar and Spice:
You can coat the rim of each mug with crushed peppermint candies! Mix together 3 tablespoons of granulated sugar with 3 tablespoons warm water and stir to dissolve. Place the sugar mixture and the crushed peppermints each into their own shallow lid, shallow saucer with a lip, or small bowl with a flat bottom. Dip the rim of the mug into the sugar water, then into the crushed peppermint candies. Fill the mugs with hot cocoa and enjoy!

CANDY POP PUNCH

Sweet as a gumdrop, but with a pop! This punch is sweet and bubbly with a gummy treat at the bottom. Jolly can't help but go searching for the gummy bears at the bottom, his favorite part!

YIELD: 10 SERVINGS

4 cups white grape juice

2 cups fruit punch

4 cups lemon-lime soda

8 to 12 ounces gummy bears, gumdrops, or other gummy candy (about 6 per glass)

10 maraschino cherries

Popping candy, for serving (optional)

In a large pitcher or punchbowl, pour the grape juice, fruit punch, and lemon-lime soda. Mix with a large spoon, then add ice if not already cold.

Add gummy candies to the bottom of clear glasses. Pour the punch over top of the gummy bears. Add a few extra gummy bears and a maraschino cherry to a stir stick or a fancy toothpick to garnish. Add a handful of popping candy (if using) to the drink right before serving. Sip and enjoy!

The NASA Apollo 9 command modulars were nicknamed gumdrops for their shape.

Green gummy bears are typically strawberry flavored, and white gummy bears are typically pineapple flavored.

SWEET COTTON CANDY SIPPER

Fluffy and sweet, cotton candy (also called cotton floss) is the perfect final topping to any party drink. King Kandy loves this fancy drink for raising a glass to CANDY LAND. Add the cotton candy right before you serve, as it dissolves into the drink quickly once it gets wet! You can also let guests pour the drink over top of cotton candy that you put in glasses before the party starts. This fruity drink is bubbly *and* fun!

YIELD: 8 SERVINGS

8 maraschino cherries

2 liters fruity soda of choice, cold

1 bag cotton candy

Fun cups and straws

Drop a maraschino cherry into the bottom of each glass. Pour the soda into each glass.

Add a fun straw, then top each glass with a generous piece of cotton candy right before serving. Sip and enjoy.

Candy Castle

ROCK CANDY FRUI-TEA

Princess Lolly has the best drink tip to make them sweet, fun, and extra fruity! Add rock candy stir sticks to herbal fruit tea. Party guests can swirl the sticks in their drinks! This quick and easy idea looks as pretty as it tastes and is a delicious touch of fun to any celebration.

YIELD: 4 SERVINGS

4 herbal fruit tea bags (berry teas work well)

4 rock candies on sticks

Pour hot water into four mugs. Add a tea bag to each mug. Steep the tea by gently pulling on the tea bag string.

Serve with a stick of rock candy, instructing guests to stir the tea until sweetened to taste. As the rock candy dissolves, it will sweeten the tea.

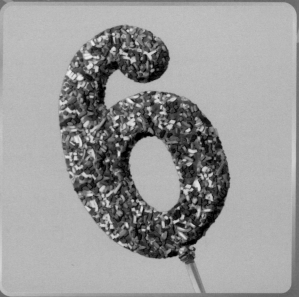

CHAPTER 7:
PRINCESS LOLLY'S PARTY AND DECORATION TIPS

Invite all of your family and friends to Princess Lolly's CANDY LAND party, and let's have a blast! These ideas will help you turn your party area into a sweet space with a sprinkle of extra fun. Try decorating with giant candies, making your lips sparkle with sprinkles, and serving your treats in some of the sweetest ways. This is exactly how Princess Lolly brings a touch of fun and a bit of CANDY LAND sweetness to every one of her parties.

HOW TO THROW A CANDY LAND PARTY

A CANDY LAND party can be as fancy or as simple as you like. From the decorations to sweet snacks and treats to games, your CANDY LAND party will be a blast from beginning to end. Use the tips from Princess Lolly in this chapter, and the recipes you've learned throughout the others, to plan your amazing CANDY LAND adventure!

LOCATION, LOCATION, LOCATION!

When Princess Lolly is throwing a party, she starts by thinking about the location for the party and how many friends she will invite to the celebration. Consider the amount of space you have to make sure your guests are comfortable, so they can have fun.

Princess Lolly also considers how much room is available for food and games. If you have access to a kitchen, you may be able to serve some frosty cold foods that melt, such as Ice Cream Bonbons (**page 64**). Even if you don't have a kitchen, you still need tables and any food you plan to have at the party.

The time of day you choose for the party can influence some of the ideas and food that you choose. Having a morning party might mean you use some of the breakfast recipes found in chapter 1. An afternoon or evening party may be a good time to decorate Cookie Flower Pops (**page 39**).

DECORATIONS BRING YOU TO CANDY LAND!

Once you know what space you will use, add a dash of sweetness and color with decorations that make you feel like you just walked into Candy Castle. Start by covering tables with bright tablecloths and hanging bright-colored balloons.

Next decorate your space. Try making the Giant Lollipop Party Decoration (**page 119**), which is great for outdoors or to lean against a wall indoors. Then make the Jumbo Wrapped Candy Party Decoration (**page 121**), which can float from the ceiling or hang on the walls.

Place a game board path right down a hallway or walkway, using the instructions for the CANDY LAND Game Board Decoration (**page 125**). When they arrive at the party, guests will feel like they are Gingerbread Movers, racing to the Candy Castle.

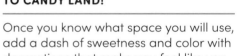

Peanut butter cups have such a magical taste because the smoothness and sweetness of the chocolate and the slight crunchiness and saltiness of the peanut butter contrast each other when you eat them.

MAKE SWEET PARTY SNACKS AND NIBBLES

For Princess Lolly, the hardest part of planning any party is picking the perfect sweets to serve! Use these tips to narrow down the choices to find the perfect snacks.

Start by picking two to three treats you love. Think about food sensitivities the guests may have, and where you will store and serve the treats.

- **Celebrating a birthday:** Make the Sprinkle Explosion Cake **(page 42)** or the Rainbow Cupcakes **(page 44)**!

- **Party outside:** Set up a s'mores station for an outside party, and make Peanut Butter Cup S'mores **(page 31)**. You can also set out a tray with some of the other variation ideas to try listed in that recipe. Don't forget a firepit and marshmallow roasting sticks!

- **Have a tea party:** Make Rock Candy Frui-tea **(page 113)**. The Mini Double Chocolate Raspberry Tarts **(page 52)** and the Choco-Lot Butter Cookies **(page 29)** are the perfect treats for a sweet tea party!

- **Perfect for a crowd:** Set up the Sprinkle Strawberry Brownie Cones **(page 83)** as a serve-yourself station, so guests can add their favorite toppings. The Jubilee Cheesecake Bars recipe **(page 68)** makes a large amount of finger food–size treats that are colorful and perfect for sharing. Jolly's Easy Party Trail Mix **(page 89)** is also a great idea to satisfy the sweet tooth when you have a larger party.

SWEET PARTY GAMES

Lastly, you'll need some fun CANDY LAND–themed activities and games for your guests! Whether you're into taking goofy selfies to remember your party or playing silly games, you have to try these ideas. Here are a few of Princess Lolly's favorite ways to party with her guests.

- **Play Princess Lolly's musical chairs:** Use candy-themed songs and set up chairs in a circle with seats facing outward so you have one less chair than the number of people who are playing. Play the music and have everyone walk in circles around the chairs. When you stop the music, everyone finds a chair. The person who doesn't find a chair becomes King Kandy's DJ and stops the music next time.

- **Plan a candy-making group activity:** Make Candy Kabobs **(page 126)** with your guests. Supply lots of different options so your guests can make unique treats. The Sour Gummy Bear Scepters **(page 77)** are another fun one to make with a group!

- **Have a relay race:** Race with a large gumdrop or marshmallow on a spoon, then pass it to the next player.

TIME TO PARTY

Get ready for a sweet adventure—your party will be so much fun! Find more party ideas and details for how to create an amazing party full of pop, sparkle, and sprinkles on the following pages!

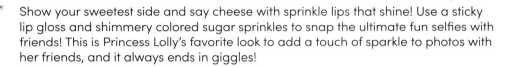

SPRINKLE LIPS

Show your sweetest side and say cheese with sprinkle lips that shine! Use a sticky lip gloss and shimmery colored sugar sprinkles to snap the ultimate fun selfies with friends! This is Princess Lolly's favorite look to add a touch of sparkle to photos with her friends, and it always ends in giggles!

1 plate with a lip per person

1 tablespoon colored sugar sprinkles per person

1 lip gloss per person (the stickier the better!)

Cotton swabs

Cotton pads, for removing makeup

Mirror

There are five main types of sprinkles that are differentiated by shape: jimmies (small, short, tube shaped), nonpareils (small, round), quins (flat, various shapes), dragees (also known as sugar pearls), sanding sugar (tiny colored sugar), and coarse sugar (thicker sugar crystals).

Put the plate on a table and add the sprinkles. The plate must have a lip around the edge to keep them from rolling everywhere.

Apply the lip gloss to your lips.

Holding the plate carefully, press your lips into the sprinkles. It can be helpful to press once in the center and then to do each side separately.

Use the cotton swaps and the cotton pads to remove any excess sugar. The cotton pads can also be used to remove the sugar when you are finished enjoying your shiny lips.

Snap some photos with your friends!

BONUS! Sugar and Spice:
The type of sprinkles you use matters a lot. Larger sprinkles will have a harder time staying on your lips. The tiny round ball sprinkles tend to bleed the color a lot. Stick to colored sugar for best results!

GIANT LOLLIPOP PARTY DECORATION

Making giant lollipops always brings a smile to Princess Lolly's face! Make one or a dozen of these adorable giant lollipops to add to any party space.

Pool noodles

Colored duct tape in contrasting colors

Hot glue gun and glue

PVC pipe or long dowel rod at least 48 inches tall

Sharp scissors

1 roll clear cellophane wrap

Large wide ribbon

Starting at the top of the pool noodle, use the colored duct tape to make a wide spiral stripe down the pool noodle. When you're finished, the pool noodle should look similar to a candy cane without the hook.

Turn on the hot glue gun. Starting at one end of the pool noodle, roll the pool noodle, using the hot glue to secure it as you go. You may need to pause as you work your way down the pool noodle to allow the glue to dry. Also be careful not to push the hot glue gun into the pool noodle or it may melt the pool noodle. Continue working your way down the pool noodle, securing it with hot glue until it is a giant twisted lollipop shape!

Push the PVC pipe into the lollipop to help you measure how big the hole should be. Then use the scissors to cut a hole that's the same size as the PVC pipe. Add more hot glue to attach the candy to the handle. Secure anything loose with hot glue then allow everything to dry fully.

Use the cellophane to cover the giant lollipop. Use the ribbon to secure the cellophane and tie a big bow. Then enjoy your decoration!

JUMBO WRAPPED CANDY PARTY DECORATION

Create a candy wonderland with bright, colorful candy decorations that will bring some sweetness to your party space! You can make as many as you want, and they will add a pop of color and fun to any room that is fit for Queen Frostine!

Acrylic paint

Small paint brushes

5 to 10 cardboard tubes, such as paper towel or toilet paper tubes

5 to 10 paper plates (solid color preferred)

40 clear mini elastic hairbands

1 roll clear cellophane wrap

Bamboo skewers (optional)

Clear string or ribbon (optional)

Using the acrylic paint and paint brushes, paint the toilet paper tubes in different bright colors, then let them dry. Add dashes or polka dots in another color to look like sprinkles.

Paint the paper plates to look like peppermint candy and other hard candy with swirls. Use the white side of the plate, then add colorful swirls all in one color. Or use a solid-colored plate and paint white swirls. Get creative with colors!

Once the paint is dry, cut pieces of clear cellophane wrap that are long enough to wrap the candy decorations. Twist the ends of the cellophane on each end and secure each with a clear hairband.

For the round candies, it can sometimes be tricky to get the cellophane to stick out on the ends depending on how wide your roll of cellophane is. To help the candy lay properly, slide a bamboo skewer (if using) through the hairbands on the back of the candy.

Decorate your candy wonderland! Hang the candies so that the unpainted side faces the wall. The long candies made of cardboard tubes can be hung along the wall or hung from clear string (if using) from the ceiling.

The largest candy cane was made in 2012 in Chicago and was fifty-one feet long.

CANDY CANE TASTE TEST GAME

Candy canes come in so many flavors! Mayor Mint loves his magical peppermint but knows everyone has their own perfect flavor. At your next party, try this game and see if you can stump your family and friends.

4 to 5 candy canes in various flavors and colors

Blindfolds or bandanas

Timer

Unwrap all of the candy canes and place similar flavors in the same container with a lid before playing the game.

Have all the players place a blindfold or bandana over their eyes. Give each player a candy cane on a plate. Set a timer for 15 seconds and allow each player to smell and taste the candy cane while blindfolded. At the end of the 15 seconds, have each player guess the flavor, then tell them the right flavor.

Keep track of who guesses the correct flavor of candy canes, and at the end announce the winners!

Peppermint tops the charts as the number one flavor for nonchocolate hard candies, as it is used both as candy and to freshen your breath.

While most candy canes are peppermint flavored, you can find all kinds of flavors including pizza, pickle, blueberry, mac and cheese, cinnamon, root beer, gravy, and birthday cake.

BONUS! Sugar and Spice:
Candy canes come in lots of flavors from traditional, such as peppermint and chocolate, to fun, such as sour apple. To really stump your guests, try to find at least one unusual flavor of candy cane. Pickle, mac and cheese, sour lemon—see if you can trick your party guests and the giggles are sure to start!

HOW TO SERVE CANDY LAND CUPCAKES

When cupcakes are served in the Candy Castle, Princess Lolly makes sure it is with much celebration! Serve cupcakes the same way they do at the Candy Castle by giving your guests a little sweet treat surprise under their cupcake!

Colorful candy, such as gummies, gumballs, chocolates, or hard candies

5-ounce tumbler cups

Cupcakes of choice

Vanilla is often added to white chocolate for flavoring.

Pour about 1 inch of colorful candy into each cup. The candy allows the cupcake to a little higher in the cup, making it easier for guests to reach. You want the bottom of the frosting to be about in line or slightly higher than the rim of the cup when you fill the cup with candy.

Place a cupcake in the cup. This tumbler style cup is usually 2¾ inches across and about 2¼ inches tall. A standard size cupcake is usually 2 to 2½ inches across and 2 to 2½ inches tall, depending on how much frosting is on it.

Serve and enjoy!

SPRINKLE NUMBER CAKE TOPPER

Celebrate someone's special day with a colorful chocolate cake topper made just for them! Write a number or initials in chocolate, then coat in colorful sprinkles for an edible cake topper that has all of CANDY LAND jumping with excitement!

1 cup chocolate chips

½ tablespoon shortening, vegetable oil, or coconut oil

¼ cup lightweight sprinkles, such as jimmies or quins

Chocolate sprinkles are called jimmies, but rainbow-colored jimmies are common, too.

Line a baking sheet with parchment paper. Place a strong zip-top bag into a tall glass, opening and folding the top over the outside of the glass.

Place the chocolate chips and the shortening in a small microwave-safe bowl. Melt the chocolate in 20- to 30-second increments in the microwave, stirring between each one, until the chocolate is smooth, 2 to 3 minutes total.

Pour the melted chocolate into the zip-top bag in the glass. Close the bag, gently pushing the chocolate down to one corner.

Take the chocolate to the parchment paper. Carefully snip a ¼-inch-wide hole in the corner of the bag with the corner turned up (the chocolate will be a bit drippy and will come out of the bag quickly).

With the chocolate, write a large block number or letter that is about 5 inches high and at least 3 inches wide. Make sure your lines are ½- to 1-inch-wide lines. Leave lots of space between the chocolate lines as the chocolate will spread a little. You may have to go over the lines more than once to make the lines wide enough and shaped how you like.

Immediately add one to two lollipop or ice pop sticks in your number or letter. Add a little more melted chocolate on top of the sticks to make sure they are well covered.

Cover the chocolate with the sprinkles.

Place the baking sheet in the freezer for 30 to 60 minutes, or until the chocolate fully sets. Once set, carefully remove the number or letter from the parchment paper. Place on top of a cake!

CANDY LAND GAME BOARD DECORATION

Make party guests feel like they are walking right into their own magical CANDY LAND! Create your own board game pathway as a decoration to make your space feel extra enchanted!

White aisle runner (optional)

Masking tape or double-sided tape

Large squares of poster board, in red, yellow, blue, and green

Find a long space with a flat surface where you can lay out the pathway. This idea works best on hardwoods, tile, vinyl, or concrete. Lay the aisle runner (if using) down through the space to define the CANDY LAND path. Attach with masking tape to the ground.

Cut the poster board into squares if not already cut. Lay the colored squares down along the path so that they are spaced evenly. Secure well with masking tape or double-sided tape.

Make this path with smaller squares of paper if you do not use the aisle runner. Use a thicker paper, such as colored cardstock, if using paper squares.

CANDY KABOBS

How many different combinations of candy shapes and colors can you come up with? King Kandy loves to find the most fun shapes and colors of gummies to add to his candy kabobs! If you have one of his kabobs, you might have a gummy shark next to a slice of gummy watermelon all next to a big gummy bear!

2 to 3 bags of gummies in various shapes and flavors

10 to 12 bamboo sticks

Clear cellophane wrap (optional)

Ribbon (optional)

Add gummies to a bamboo stick to make easy candy kabobs. Pick gummy candies that have interesting shapes, such as hearts, watermelons, or cherries.

Hand the kabobs out as treats or as party favors: Wrap them in clear cellophane (if using; see the Jumbo Wrapped Candy Party Decoration on page 121), using ribbon to secure the cellophane with a bow.

BONUS! Sugar and Spice: Make your kabobs sour! Use the technique described in the Sour Gummy Bear Scepters recipe on page 77.

AUTHOR DEDICATION

To my husband, Noel, and my daughter, Hailey, who always make everything more fun, especially time together in the kitchen. Life is extra sweet with the love and support of my favorite taste testers and cheerleaders.

INSIGHT EDITIONS

PO Box 3088
San Rafael, CA 94912
www.insighteditions.com

Find us on Facebook: www.facebook.com/InsightEditions
Follow us on Twitter: @insighteditions

ISBN: 978-1-64722-521-6

Publisher: Raoul Goff
VP of Licensing and Partnerships: Vanessa Lopez
VP of Creative: Chrissy Kwasnik
VP of Manufacturing: Alix Nicholaeff
VP, Editorial Director: Vicki Jaeger
Art Director, Kids: Stuart Smith
Designer: Brooke McCullum
Editor: Anna Wostenberg
Editorial Assistant: Elizabeth Ovieda
Managing Editor: Maria Spano
Senior Production Editor: Katie Rokakis
Production Associate: Deena Hashem
Senior Production Manager, Subsidiary Rights: Lina s Palma-Temena

Illustrations by Ilaria Vescovo and Paulo Borges

ROOTS of PEACE   REPLANTED PAPER

Insight Editions, in association with Roots of Peace, will plant two trees
for each tree used in the manufacturing of this book. Roots of Peace is
an internationally renowned humanitarian organization dedicated to
eradicating land mines worldwide and converting war-torn lands into
productive farms and wildlife habitats. Roots of Peace will plant two
million fruit and nut trees in Afghanistan and provide farmers there with
the skills and support necessary for sustainable land use.

Manufactured in China by Insight Editions

10 9 8 7 6 5 4 3 2 1